"SHUT UP AND GET IN LINE!"

Catherine Walsh

Mystical Rose Press

"SHUT UP AND GET IN LINE!"
By Catherine Walsh

Cover Art by Jared Giangiulio

No part of this publication may be reproduced, stored in a retrieval system or transmitted in any form or by any means, electronic, mechanical or otherwise without the written permission of the Publisher. All rights reserved.

Published in the United States of America
First Published 2009

ISBN 978-0-578-01163-9

Ad Majorem Dei Gloriam

In gratitude to all Priests, Nuns and Religious for teaching the Faith.

Table of Contents

INTRODUCTION	1
1. OPENING LINES	3
2. TRAVELLING ALONG PARALLEL LINES	6
3. TOW THE LINE	17
4. WALKING A STRAIGHT LINE	20
5. GOD'S TIMELINE	27
6. IMAGINARY LINES	31
7. FALL IN LINE	34
8. LINE OF SUCCESSION	37
9. IN LINE WITH HIS WILL	39
10. CROSSING THE LINE	41
11. WELCOMING LINE	47
12. THE BATTLE LINES ARE DRAWN	50
13. LINE 'EM UP	55
14. CRYSTALLINE MEMORIES	58
15. A LONG LINE OF RELATIVES	65
16. GOD WRITES STRAIGHT WITH OUR CROOKED LINES	67
17. GOD'S PLUMB LINE	74
18. SAFETY LINE	77
19. IN THE LINE OF FIRE	81
20. SCARY MOVIE LINES	84
21. IN THE LINE OF DUTY	88
22. LINE OF DEMARCATION	93
23. SMILE LINES	98
24. EVERY CLOUD HAS A SILVER LINING	103
25. SETTING BOUNDARY LINES	106
26. TOP OF THE LINE FASHION FOR THE IN-CROWD	109
27. FORBIDDEN LINE	112
28. ON THE FRONT LINES	116
29. FALLING HOOK, LINE AND SINKER	126
30. PRECIOUS BLOODLINE	127

31. OUR LIFELINE	132
32. OFFENSIVE LINES	137
33. LINE OF ACTION	141
34. WHAT'S MY LINE?	147
35. A REWARDING LINE OF WORK	148
36. DROPPING JAWLINES	152
37. ARE YOU NEXT IN LINE?	153
38. RUN STRAIGHT FOR THE GOAL LINE	156
39. CONNECTING LINES	167
40. LINING UP TO SAY THANK YOU	171
41. BROKEN LINES OF COMMUNICATION	176
42. CROSSING THE FINISH LINE	178
NOTES	188

INTRODUCTION

Ecclesiastes 3:1 tells us, "For everything there is a season and a time for every purpose under Heaven."

We can see from Holy Scripture that our lives are constantly changing. Sometimes, our feelings can quickly turn from happy and joyful to serious and thoughtful. "A time to laugh - a time to cry, a time to live - a time to die."

(Eccles.3:1)

Even in the course of one day, our lives can go from the profound to the ridiculous and back again. As one who loves to laugh, I recognize the need in all of us for Laughter and Joy. God has given us these gifts and I believe it makes Him happy when we use them. He has also given us Wisdom and Prudence to seek after and discover the deep and esoteric truths which we need in order to reach our eternal home.

Our perfectly ordered and designed world is a reflection of its perfect Creator. As His creatures, made in His image and likeness, we must order our lives in complete conformity to His will and learn to walk the straight and narrow path that leads to Heaven's door.

Having heard the call to His Service, thousands of dedicated priests and sisters have trained generations of school children, taught them the importance of living according to God's Laws and have passed onto them the knowledge and beauty of the Holy Catholic Church.

Those of us who attended Catholic School have had some similar experiences. We all have our own childhood memories, and depending on the years we attended, our family situations, nationalities, and geographical location, our memories may be somewhat different. However, there are certain commonalities in Catholic parish life with which we can all identify.

Our lives are full of the profound and the ridiculous. So too is this book. On these pages are humorous memories of bygone schooldays, but also enlightening Scripture verses and quotes from the Saints. I have included certain stories to give the reader insight into the world of a young child growing up in an Irish Catholic family. The nineteen-fifties and sixties are the times and Levittown, Pennsylvania in the suburban parish of Saint Joseph the Worker is the place. Some of the names have been changed to protect the guilty and the innocent.

Our attitudes and perspectives on things can change over the years (Praise God) and our memories can fade, but the One, Holy, Catholic and Apostolic Church which is rooted in our Triune, unchanging God, will stand until the end of time and the gates of hell will not prevail against it.

Chapter 1

"OPENING LINES"
A New School Year Begins

We could sense that our cherished vacation days were drawing to an end and a new school year was upon us. Our thrilling games of "Keep Away," "Red Rover," and "Tag," would have to be put on hold until after school. Warm summer evenings filled with our favorite past-times would be replaced with homework and early bedtimes. No longer would we be making clover necklaces or lightning bug rings. We wouldn't be jumping on our bikes to follow the "Mosquito Man" in his pesticide truck. We would miss riding to our hearts content in the thick cloud of DDT smoke that was both putrid and sweet smelling at the same time. I can still hear the gleeful screams of the neighborhood kids, and my brother's bragging voice rising up from the dense fog, "Look at me! I'm right in the middle of it! I left you in the dust!"

Worst of all, the ice cream man would not be coming back again this season. (This was the late fifties and sixties. After our black and white television sets warmed up, we could turn on one of our favorite shows. Leave it to Beaver, I Love Lucy, the Mickey Mouse Club and Queen for a Day were high on our list. The raciest thing on TV was The Dick Van

Dyke Show. We were overjoyed to be getting our first Catholic President and our memories seemed frozen in time a few short years later when President Kennedy was assassinated. A bold new singing group called the Beatles captured our attention on the Ed Sullivan Show and really pushed the boundaries of good taste. We held our breaths when they announced the winner in the national contest naming the Flintstones baby, "Pebbles."

Children began receiving vaccinations against polio with Dr. Salk's new vaccine.

Golden arches were added to the American landscape when a new restaurant called McDonalds offered us fifteen cent burgers.

The post World War II Baby Boom filled the sixties with seventy-million teenagers and these youth swayed fashion, fads and the politics of the decade.

Teenagers could listen to their favorite records on their very own transistor radios complete with earphones, or play them at home on their high-fidelity record players. They danced to the Twist, Mashed Potato and the Bristol Stomp while watching American Bandstand.

We would all watch in amazement as we saw Neal Armstrong take his first step onto the surface of the moon.

Our mothers stayed home and took care of the house and the whole family ate supper together when the dads came home from work.

A "school shooter" was the kid who threw spitballs across the room and the most daring thing we ever did was to knock on doors and disappear in a hilarious fit of laughter.)

We would be leaving behind our hula hoops, balls, erector sets and dolls. We would have to turn off the sprinklers that we ran through all summer, and the keys that hung around our necks to adjust our metal

Shut Up and Get in Line

skates would have to come off. No more drinks from the hose or Hide and Seek at dusk. No more running until we were tired or laughing until our stomachs hurt and we couldn't breathe. All of our beloved toys would be waiting for us at home while we were trapped in a classroom for another school year. We knew where we were headed and what we must do. Still, with the sadness of saying goodbye to our summer fun, there was always a tinge of excitement surrounding the new adventure that lay before us. We would soon be leaving our fond memories behind and our thoughts and minds would be headed once again back to school.

Chapter 2

"TRAVELLING ALONG PARALLEL LINES"
Our Similar School Experiences

Our imaginations ran wild with anticipation, anxiety and excitement. What kind of school year would we have? Who would we get? (Translation- Who would our new teacher be?) What if she's mean? What if she makes us do long division? What if we have to sit next to a bad kid or a dirty kid? A frightful series of "what if's" led to a new world of possibilities opening up for us. What if we were one of the lucky ones who were assigned one of the important jobs, such as carrying Sister's books from the convent to the school, washing the blackboards, or writing the names of the "talkers" on the board? Perhaps we would be chosen to hold the lavatory door or be given the responsibility of flushing all the toilets after the girls were through.

With any luck, I could be the one who holds the water fountain while the class gets their drink- one, two, three, OFF! No one could question or dispute the three second rule. I would be in charge, and when I turned that faucet off, it is done. Move on! Silence would prevail. There would be no comments made, period. Yes, that is the job I wanted, and power driven or not, that is the one for which I would be

Shut Up and Get in Line

praying.

There was only one job that I would not want. But, oh no! What if by some fluke, I was to be assigned that job?! It was the one that Leonard always had. When someone threw up, or to use the proper and classier term, regurgitate, (which usually happened on the first day of school or whenever there was a big test), the teacher would yell, "Leonard!" and poor Leonard always ran for the bucket and mop and helped the teacher clean it up. He was the bravest boy in our class and everyone admired him.

Everyone took turns with the "Call Cards." The Sisters and Teachers made up a stack of cards with the names of the students on them. Each student would get a chance to call names from the stack to answer questions. Depending on the subject matter we were studying, you either dreaded or looked forward to having your name called. Sometimes, if you got lucky, you could signal to a willing card caller whether to call you or not. Since the nuns had eyes in the back of their heads, this could be a very risky maneuver. Besides which, it could backfire on you if the card caller took it upon himself to teach you a lesson on ethics. Then you would be hung out to dry. Sitting their clueless and stunned like a deer in the headlights, you vowed never to bother the card dealer again. You would fare better by taking your chances with the luck of the draw and just hope your name didn't turn up next.

Math was my least favorite subject. I think I can pinpoint the exact year when I turned into a math moron. Our third grade teacher told us to write the word Arithmetic in our copybooks. Apparently some students had trouble spelling that big word. Sister said to remember this sentence- "A rat in Tom's house may eat Tom's ice cream." Well, I thought that was so cool! Even though I knew how to spell Arithmetic, this new game threw me for a loop. I thought that it was great that there was a fun new way to remember how to spell words. There was just no telling where this could go. It would open up a flood-gate of new ideas and fodder for the imagination of any kid who wasn't playing with a full deck. I was in my glory! Before I got sidetracked with that, however, I had to dwell on Tom and his poor situation. I could vaguely hear Sister's voice in the background saying something about numbers, as I wondered how the rat got into Tom's house. What did it look like? I had never seen a real rat! Did Tom know the rat was there? What kind of ice cream did Tom have? Could it be chocolate marshmallow or maybe another one of my favorites, a creamsicle? Hey, would the ice cream man be coming around anymore even though summer is over? Maybe on warm days? Well, you can see where this is going. There's an old Rodgers and Hammerstein song that says, "Do I love you because you're beautiful, or are you beautiful because I love you?" In my case it was, "Do I have trouble with math because I'm thinking of ice cream, or am I thinking of ice cream because I have trouble with math?"

I mortally detested Drill and Mental. This consisted of going down the rows and solving the arithmetic problems orally and instantly. If you stalled or the class sensed that you were wasting time, their collective voice would jump in and drag out in a sing-song fashion, "TOOOOO SLOW!" and then the class said the answer. When it was your turn and you said the wrong answer, the class was on the case, ready and waiting to sing in unison, COR-REC'-TION! - and always with a LOUD accent on the second syllable. The class would show no mercy for the late, the lazy or the inept. "Aww, dry up," I thought. I didn't care what the show offs were singing. I just glared at them and went back to thinking about my ice cream. When I was paying attention and knew the answer, I was the first to sing the loudest and with the most enthusiasm, "TOOOOO SLOW!" or "COR-REC-TION!" I always had the feeling that I could have done better in math if I could just study my times tables that were literally at my fingertips on the back cover of my black and white marble copybook, but we were forbidden to look back there. School life in the fifties and sixties came with another unique set of challenges. We were experiencing the Cold War and the Cuban Missile Crisis. Our teachers often talked about Khrushchev and we had visions of Khrushchev marching down the street at any second to come and get us. Still, with all the fears and nightmares about Communism and Khrushchev, I always preferred the Air Raid Drills over the Arithmetic Drills. We were often corralled in the hallway to practice for the possibility of a Communist attack. We would lie flat on our stomachs with our left hand covering our eyes, so that we would not be blinded by the explosion of fire. With our right hand, we were to support our necks. This was to prevent our necks from breaking when the building fell on us. Try as he might, Khrushchev was not going to get us. We knew how to protect ourselves and we had mastered the tricks that would keep us safe. There would be no broken necks or damaged eyes at Saint Joseph the Worker School. We were one step ahead of him. (We certainly weren't the only school practicing survival tactics for nuclear war. Children all over the country were learning "to duck and cover.")

Even if something catastrophic were to happen on the way home from school, we would have been fine. We had the Safeties. When our parents or teachers weren't there, the Safeties were our elders. They knew how to take care of us because they wore a Safety badge. That badge carried with it all the authority, power and wisdom of a real adult, and we just couldn't wait for the day when we would finally wear the coveted badge ourselves. We also knew that the day we put on the badge, our self confidence would kick in and soar. The big, bad, eighth grade Safety Patrol was able to defend the entire school against everything from a public school bully to a nuclear attack, but they didn't have the guts to say "hi" to a Safety of the opposite sex.

The whole school went to Mass on first Fridays. Sister would remind us all week to be prepared for Mass and to bring our chapel veils or beanies for our heads. Invariably there would be someone who forgot. We would pass the Kleenex to the girl who forgot and she would wear a tissue on her head with a bobby pin. I always thought the tissues looked so out of place and clashed with the uniform. The "tissue heads" made all of us look bad. They ruined the appearance of the class because then we didn't have that over-all uniform look, all pressed and polished and matching as we walked into church in our lines.

If you forgot your Rosary, it was alright. Sister reassured us, "Why do you think you have ten fingers?"

We learned the correct and precise gestures and church behaviors and we did not deviate from them. We were to keep our hands folded with our fingers pointing up and our thumbs overlapping making a little cross. When we genuflected, we had better get that knee down to the ground and show proper reverence. When kneeling, we were completely straight up. If you were leaning back on the pew, you better have had two broken legs and a pair of crutches next to you.

On rainy days, we stayed inside for recess and after lunch we played "Seven Up!" Sometimes, the entire class would have a silent recess. I was the type of nitwit who would carry on and laugh during silent recess, and then when the teacher came back, I told on everyone that I

Shut Up and Get in Line

saw talking.

The best thing that could happen to a kid in the winter was to wake up and see the earth blanketed in snow. Glued to the radio, the suspense was killing us as we listened for the name of our school to be announced. Saint Joseph the Worker- Closed. Yippee! A Snow Day! A free day of fun and frolicking in the snow! We would spend most of the day outdoors making snowmen, igloos and snow angels. When our mittens were soaked and our scarves were frozen with ice balls, we wore socks on our hands. If we got thirsty outside, we reached for a two foot long icicle that was hanging from the house. Sometimes we would snap off the smaller ones from under the cars and suck on them.

After my dad finished putting the chains on the tires, he would often drive us to the lake to go ice-skating. My skates were adjustable, so I could wear them from the time I was eight until I was sixteen. After that, having two blades on each skate was no longer socially acceptable. That's when I hung up my skates for good. Besides, I wasn't even going to try to balance myself on one little blade.

We could throw all the snowballs we wanted on snow days, (as long as it didn't get back to the school), but if it was a school day, it didn't matter if you were in your own neighborhood or not, there was no touching the snow! Not with your hand, your glove, your ruler- absolutely no contact would be made between you and the snow- Period.

We learned never to waste- Anything! - Food, paper, time, etc. One day, one of our nuns acted as if she had discovered gold in the trash can. "What is this?" Sister asked, as she fished out a half-eaten peanut butter and jelly sandwich complete with teeth marks. "Who had peanut butter and jelly for lunch today?" Most of the class raised their hands. Sister moaned, "Oh, the poor little children in the missions of China who would love to have this." Sister was truly burdened with anxiety. Pacing back and forth, her clicking Rosary beads called us all to attention. I thought she would die of a broken heart. "Never again! Never again!" Sister warned us. That's all we had to hear. There would be no more food thrown away in our classroom waste basket.

When it came to paper, we used every square inch. We folded our lined loose-leaf papers in half, so we were able to fit four Spelling tests on one paper. Fridays were test days and we were tested in all of our subjects. If we were getting a timed test, we waited until Sister looked at her stop watch and announced, "BEGIN!" Heaven help the sorry soul who was still writing when Sister said, "PENCILS DOWN!"

In fifth grade we experienced a monumental rite of passage. The buildup for this event went on for months and the overwhelming anticipation was almost more than we could bear. We were getting our very own brand new Schaeffer ink-cartridge pens! Sister gave us methodical step-by-step instructions on the care and use of our superb new pens. Writing was a form of art and our cursive handwriting looked spectacular in the new, beautiful, blue ink. There was usually some poor slob (always a boy), who had a big ugly ink blotch on his nice shirt or his paper, or all over his hands! I did not understand how this could have happened. If he just would have followed Sister's clear instructions, he wouldn't be such a mess!

When I was growing up, the lines were clearly drawn, The Catholic School Kids and the Public School Kids, Us and Them, Good vs. Evil. We weren't there when the rivalry began. We inherited it from stories of the kids that went before us. We passed the public school bus stops and had witnessed firsthand their undisciplined lives. They did not have their school bags and lunch boxes neatly lined up one after the other. What were they thinking? If someone walking by accidentally kicked their lunchbox, their whole thermos could break! They didn't even board the bus one at a time in an orderly fashion, but seemed to just all jam in. They never had any homework and their Reader friends weren't John, Jean and Judy. So you just tell me how they were going to learn good Christian family values like we did. They were allowed to throw snowballs and they did not wear a uniform to school. We all knew what that meant- They probably went to school dirty and disheveled with uncombed hair. But they did have a gymnasium, swings, seesaws, sliding boards, and monkey bars, so we had visions of them playing all day or flying across the room from the ceilings. (Our "playground" was the parking lot. The rule was to stay on the blacktop, where some kids lost their brand new big front teeth. We were NEVER to go on the grass.)

They threw spitballs at one another! How obscene is that?! (If a catholic school kid was crazy enough to pull a dumb stunt like that, he would be gone before afternoon prayers, and never heard of again.)

We knew that they didn't learn a thing, and how could they? Their textbooks were not even covered! How could they concentrate when they were so disorganized? They were allowed to dot their I's with little hearts! What kind of nonsense was that? How could they focus on their work when they didn't wear uniforms? That would defy the rules of common sense. They would naturally be distracted by looking at everyone's outfits. We, on the other hand, wore a brown wool uniform jumper with starched tan blouses and the boys wore creased pants and ties. This would insure that we were not distracted and guarantee our success in life. The uniforms bore the gold emblem of SJW and each time the uniform was donned we were representing Saint Joseph the Worker School to the world. This responsibility weighed heavily on our judgmental little shoulders. We would always show the world the epitome of goodness, kindness and holiness,- except when we saw a public school kid on the street. Then we would stick out our tongues.

Yes, the general consensus was that the public school kids were rowdy and totally out of control. In fact, over the years, our parents sometimes threatened that if we did not shape up, we would land in public school because "they had to take everybody."

One morning in fifth grade, all of my judgments of public school kids were confirmed. Our class had just filed in from the playground after the morning bell. We were busy unpacking our books and hadn't even visited the cloak room, when we heard a loud gasp from one of the girls. "What is it, Mary Grace?" Sister questioned. "Sister, someone scribbled all over my desk!" I sat two rows over but I had a good vantage point for viewing the desecrated desk. There were shrieks and exclamations of "Oh No!" going up all over the classroom at the horror of it all. We all knew that the C.C.D. kids had been there the night before. Our desks were not sitting on the floor lines one behind the other as they normally were. We also knew that heads would roll. What kind of insane mind would destroy furniture which was the property of the Archdiocese of Philadelphia? This had to be the work of a deranged soul. Mary Grace was on the verge of tears. Although she was only the "Messenger" of bad tidings, there was always the outside chance that she would be blamed for this violent attack on the desk. Sister instructed Mary Grace to go and get the Principal, Sister Denise. This was big! Sister Denise only came to our classroom to give out report cards if Father couldn't make it.

Shut Up and Get in Line

When Sister Denise came in, the two nuns quietly stared in disbelief at the scribbled desk, including the pencil groove which was filthy with caked on black lead. Then they looked at one another in silence. The two of them decided that this disgrace called for professional help. The Janitor was summoned to remove the desk for special repairs and sanitizing. We all knew that Sister Denise would track down the CCD culprit and that he would pay dearly for his mistake.

After Sister Denise left, we asked our teacher, what would become of the desk vandal. We couldn't wait to see the creep get his just due. She said, "Isn't it sad that someone doesn't even know how to respect the possessions of another?" Some of us got together in the school yard and continued the CCD discussion. I can still see our self-righteous little tongues wagging and feel the genuine concern for our public school counterparts. It was decided that nothing of value would be left in our desks when CCD would be using the room. We knew that because they didn't know the Catechism, like we did, it wasn't their fault for behaving that way. We would not tempt them to take anything and we would protect them from themselves because they didn't know any better.

We kind of felt sorry for the poor CCD kids, because in later years, they would be the ones who would fist fight, especially the girls, smoke, and write hearts with a boy and girls name inside- right on their textbook! We all knew that when they grew up, they wouldn't amount to anything. I once asked my father how come the public school kids had nicer schools, playing fields, games, a big cafeteria where you could even buy food, and their schools also had better technology? I knew from his response that he was the most caring, kind and generous Christian I had ever known- "Because," he said, "I'm paying for it all."

Maybe it did look like the public school kids had more than we did, but we had the ace in the hole, our secret weapon that would assure that we would learn come hell or high water. We had the Nuns!

Chapter 3

"TOW THE LINE"
"Be Virtuous"

Me, myself and I, that unholy trinity around which I thought the entire universe revolved. I believe I was the most greedy, selfish, and hedonistic person on earth. I realize we are all this way as babies, but for some of us, this self-centered stage is prolonged far beyond childhood.

Thank God for us that the nuns came into our lives to shape us up.

We were blessed to have gone to Catholic school. Although at times we rebelled, that good old Catholic guilt always pulled us back. The faith we were taught is undeniable and its lovely traditions became ingrained in our beings. We were fed at the table of Truth in our church and the roots of our understanding run deep into the core of our very souls.

But, why was everything so ordered and why were the nuns so strict in making sure we did everything just right? If there was a black smudge on our paper or a hole made by an eraser, the paper would be ripped up and we would have to start over. If our desks were not in order, they would be turned over and the contents dumped out for us to begin again. We may have thought at the time that it was inconsequential if we learned to live an ordered life and do things a certain way. When I reflect on my life, however, it was the discipline and self-control I learned from the nuns that always helped me in every situation. They taught us valuable lessons in how to live an upstanding and virtuous life. There were certain characteristics of the nuns that we could never forget. Besides having great faith in God, they had great faith in their students. They never gave up on us and they always made sure that we learned what they taught. They had amazing perseverance and would not accept anything that they knew was not our greatest effort. Eventually, they drew the best and brightest thoughts from our minds and we can attribute the learning of many of lifes most serious lessons to the teaching of the nuns. The nuns were looking after our souls long before we were. They tried to whip us into shape at every turn. We provided the crude raw material which had to be formed and molded into wonderful little children with good morals and social skills, strong intellects and outstanding characters.

The Catechism played a huge role in our Religious education and we were nurtured with this book throughout our Catholic school years.

To insure that our character development was progressing, we even had Report Card grades for; Obedience, Self-Control, Perseverance, Cooperation, Courage, Orderliness and Health Habits. The values and virtues which were being instilled in us as children would be etched in our psyche and would be called up to work in us and shine brightly toward the performance of good deeds.

Because the nuns expected excellence from us, nothing less would be accepted or tolerated. Thank God they did not accept shoddy, lazy, or disorganized behavior and thinking. They knew that organization and self-discipline were crucial in the teaching of truth and right reason.

These words from Holy Scripture help us to remember the nuns and give thanks to God for the discipline and self-control they taught us.

Shut Up and Get in Line

"A wooden beam can be put into a building so firmly that an earthquake cannot shake it loose; a person can be trained to use reason and good sense so well that he keeps his head when a crisis comes." A mind that thinks things through intelligently is like a firm wall finely decorated. Small stones on top of a wall will not stay put when the wind blows, and a person whose stupid ideas have made him timid will not be able to stand up to frightening situations."

Sirach 22-23

Catholic Schools were microcosms of God's orderly world and the nuns were teaching us to conform to the Holy will of our magnificent and perfect Creator.

Chapter 4

"WALKING A STRAIGHT LINE"
Conformity to God's Laws

In Catholic School there was strict enforcement of the rules, learning about the Saints, knowing your Catechism inside out, Sentence Diagramming, No Talking Ever, First Friday Masses, Pollyannas, buying Pagan Babies and the spotless keeping of your Permanent Record. But what I remember most were the Lines- the Lavatory Lines, the Playground Lines, the Bus Lines, the Car Line, the Communion Line, the Confession Line, etc. We went everywhere in lines and always with one head behind the other, hands at our sides, up straight, in silence.

We had good training for the countless other lines we would wait in during our lifetimes; the grocery line, the ticket line, the unemployment line, etc. We are forced to deal with lines throughout our whole lives. If you stop to think about it, we wait in lines from the time we are born until the time we die. When I went to the hospital to have my baby, I was told that there were two women in line ahead of me. My baby was third in line to be born that day. When he was baptized, he was fifth in a horizontal line to receive the Sacrament. We stand in line to go into the Confessional to receive the Sacrament of Penance and we file in a line when we receive the Holy Eucharist. We walk up in a line to receive the Sacraments of Matrimony and Holy Orders. Even when we die, the

Shut Up and Get in Line

faithful process in a line behind the casket.

What and Who is present in all of these Sacramental lines? The Sacrament is present, the faithful Communion of Saints in the Body of Christ is present and most importantly Christ Himself is present, Who is preparing us for eternity.

Our Lord expects us to walk with Him and live in conformity to His holy will. Saint Francis de Sales teaches us, "We cannot help conforming ourselves to what we love."[1] In the big universal scheme of things, we cannot help but get a glimpse of the awesome beauty, and perfectly ordered Mind of our wondrous Creator.

Lines symbolize order. When we want to put things in order, we arrange them in a line. There are lines everywhere in God's great universe. Observe sunrays, moonbeams, the Cross. It's intriguing to me that everything is made of lines. Look at the room you are in. Everything is either a straight, circular or curved line.

"Biblical authors, including Solomon and Paul, used the line as a metaphor to depict goodness and evil. Typically, a straight line represents goodness and obedience, while a crooked one symbolizes departure from righteousness. Solomon's famous proverb is one example: "Trust in the Lord with all your heart and lean not on your own understanding; in all your ways acknowledge Him, and He will make your paths straight." In contrast, Solomon writes in Ecclesiastes 7:29, "This only have I found: God made mankind upright but men have gone in search of many schemes." "These two verses demonstrate that God makes one's path, or life, straight and righteous, while rebellious men scorn uprightness and seek an alternate, crooked path. Paul says something similar in Philippians 2:14-15: "Do everything without complaining or arguing, so that you may become blameless and pure, children of God without fault in a crooked and depraved world." Here, crookedness and depravity are synonymous." Both the New and Old Testaments use line metaphors to discuss goodness and evil, obedience and rebellion. Lines, angles and circles are powerful metaphors because everyone understands them. We all experience these shapes in our lives, so when we encounter them in our reading, they can speak to us as metaphors."[2] Pascal, the brilliant geometrician, who also made a monumental impact on French prose said in his "Pensees"- "God is a circle whose center is everywhere, and whose circumference is nowhere."

There are countless references from Holy Scripture and religious books which stress the importance of conformity and following God's Law in order to stay on the path that leads to heaven's door. St. John the Baptist reminds us, "Make straight the way of the Lord." Matthew 7:14 tells us, "How narrow is the gate and straight is the way that leadeth to life, and few there are that find it." St. Alphonsus Liguori gives it to us straight - "All wish to be saved and enjoy the glory of Paradise; but to gain heaven, it is necessary to walk in the straight road that leads to eternal bliss."[3] So, it always turns out that when we do things our way, ignore God's Commandments and step off the straight and narrow path, disaster strikes.

Throughout Scripture the Lord teaches us using the line concept. Here are just a few examples:

> Isaiah 44:13- "The carpenter stretches a line, he marks it out with a pencil, he fashions it with planes, and marks it with a compass; he shapes it into the figure of a man with the beauty of a man to dwell in the house."

Shut Up and Get in Line

Isaiah 28:17- "Judgment also will I lay to the line."

Amos 7:7- "He showed me; behold the Lord was standing beside a wall built with a plumb line, with a plumb line in His hand."

Corinthians-1:9- "Every athlete in training submits to strict discipline, in order to be crowned with a wreath that will not last; but we do it for one that will last forever. That is why I run straight for the finish line."

Genesis-5:1- "This is the written account of Adam's line. When God created man, He made him in the likeness of God."

Nu.-34:7- "For your northern boundary, run a line from the Great Sea to Mount Hor."

1 Ki-7:15- "He cast two bronze pillars, each 18 cubits high and 12 cubits around, by line."

"Since God has enacted certain lines, limits and boundaries on His creatures, we could look at sin as crossing one of those lines that God has drawn." In the process of ignoring God's lines, one turns liberty into license and inches closer and closer to the devil's inviting flame. (Galatians 5:13-14)

As Christians, there are lines behind us, supporting us and directing us; they are lines through which we must never backslide (Hebrews 10:35-39). There are lines ahead of us, protecting us from transgressing into a realm of self-indulgence and shortsighted immorality (2 John

7-11). Wisdom dictates that we strive to maintain a sanctified equilibrium in our lives, drifting in neither direction, for both spell doom. What joy comes from being encircled by God. When He has drawn lines, observe them and uphold them for they are not burdensome compared to the weight of the cross upon our Lord's back." (Romans 7:22, 1 John 5:3)[4]

The Little Boy Who Wouldn't Get On the Bus

There was a little boy that lived on my street who was having trouble going to school. After a few days of making a scene, his mother made sure he would get on the bus and go to school. On this particular day, I was walking a good distance behind them, but I could see and hear what was happening. The mother would give him a swat on his behind and say, "What are you going to do?" The boy said, "I'm gonna get on the bus." After another few yards the mother would swat and question him again, "What are you going to do?" The boy shot back, "I'm gonna get on the bus." This went on and on every few yards like a broken record. The nearer we got to the bus stop, the louder the exchange. Frankly, the whole scene made me a little nervous. Why was the boy so frightened? What does he know that I don't know? But he was younger than I, so I figured he was just a scaredy-cat acting foolishly. I watched with great interest to see if the words he was saying were really sinking in. Finally the bus pulled up and on he went still mumbling, "I'm gonna get on the bus."

SHUT UP AND GET IN LINE!

I had a nun once who was very frustrated because the class kept talking and ignoring her directions. Sister finally shouted, "Shut up and get in line!" By today's standards, that would be a mild statement. This was out of character for Sister, but she must have been fed up with our obnoxious behavior. Sister definitely got our attention. We snapped to it and formed our perfectly straight line in a flash. Sometimes we need to hear what to do and when to do it in no uncertain terms.

Sometimes we needed to hear the crack of that yardstick that Sister carried around. If someone wasn't paying attention, she could reach clear across the room with that sucker. The whole class would jump, but, boy did we ever straighten up.

Sister whether knowingly or unknowingly was teaching us more than a lesson for that day. The importance and significance of what Sister was telling us was, literally, shut your mouth and get in line. Figuratively, the message was, Tow the line, keep your mouth shut and conform. Be silent; learn what you need to know to get to Heaven. It's not your world, and you best follow the rules!

Our parents, nuns, priests and teachers were wise. They knew that our rebellious spirits had to be broken and there were many fundamental truths that had to be planted into those little brains of ours.

When watching television shows like "Super Nanny," we can see how we need more adults like the nuns. It is shocking to see how the children are running the entire household in many homes today. They hit their parents, scream, throw things and attack their siblings. Then the parent asks timidly, "Will you please stop hitting me?" or "Please stop jumping on the dining room table?" At what point along the line did the children become the boss? It's nuts! No discipline or self-control whatsoever. Gee, if we acted like that, our parents would have wiped the floor up with us. Well, we thought they would anyway, and that was good enough to get us in line. Those parents on TV would benefit from the guidance of a strict disciplinarian like a good nun or the mother of the boy who wouldn't get on the bus.

> "When we offend those set over us, we oppose the ordinance of Him who set them over us."
>
> Pope Saint Gregory the Great

Chapter 5

"GOD'S TIMELINE"
Infinite Extension in Both Directions

There is a strong connection between God's orderly world and the orderly way in which the nuns taught us to conduct our everyday lives. The nuns were preparing us to travel the journey toward eternal life by helping us to develop right thinking. We came to a greater appreciation and love of God through the manifestation of His sublime creation.

Many things concerning the nature of God are outside the realm of our human understanding. Because God exists outside of time, the concept that He always was, always will be and always remains the same is one of the great mysteries of our faith. "The desire for God is written in the human heart, because man is created by God and for God; and God never ceases to draw man to Himself. Only in God will he find the truth and happiness he never stops searching for."[1]

As St. Paul says of the Gentiles: For what can be known about God is plain to them because God has shown it to them. Ever since the creation of the world His invisible nature, namely, His eternal power and deity, has been clearly perceived in the things that have been made.[2]

"And St. Augustine issues this challenge: Question the beauty of the earth, question the beauty of the sea, question the beauty of the air distending and diffusing itself, question the beauty of the sky...question all of these realities. All respond: "See, we are beautiful." Their beauty is a profession. These beauties are subject to change. Who made them if not the Beautiful One who is not subject to change?"[3]

Father John Laux, M.A. writes on The Existence of God:

"We only have to look around us to see that the universe is full of natural works of art which in beauty, variety, grandeur, and perfection far surpass the highest achievements of human craftsmanship. Beauty is present everywhere in nature. Whether we look at the sky above us, or at the earth below, or at the wide expanse of waters, all manifest it. They display it in all their parts and under all their aspects. It is seen in the smallest flower, no less than in the forest as a whole: in the icebound regions of the pole, and in the sandy deserts, as in the glories of the tropics. Nor is it color alone that is in question. The forms of nature possess the same quality. The outlines of the different trees, the configuration of their leaves, the varied curves of their branches are as perfect in their way as is the coloring of the flowers. Of the innumerable species of animals which people earth and air and sea there is hardly one which does not arouse our wondering admiration, some by their grace, some, like the lion and the elephant, by their grandeur. Moreover, the sense of hearing, no less than that of sight, acknowledges the perfection of nature's handiwork. The song of the birds, the music of the waters, the sound of the breeze among the trees attract and delight us. We recognize beauty as the authentic note of nature in all its works."[4]

(Joyce, Principles of Natural Theology, p.127)

Shut Up and Get in Line

God's orderly and spectacular world never ceases to amaze me. The beauty of His awesome creation is in the line, design, form and colors. His creation is not only lovely to behold, but remarkably perfect in its essence. Sirach-43:11 tells us, "Look at the rainbow and praise it's Creator. How magnificent, how radiant it's beauty! Like a bow by the hands of the Most High, it spans the horizon in a circle of glory."

All of the perfections of our Heavenly Father are beyond our human understanding. Because He has created an amazingly ordered universe and has ordained our lives and their outcome for the good, all we need to do is trust and follow His Divine will and directions. When reflecting on the blessings which are received by conforming ourselves to God's will in our lives and doing things His way, the sheer logic of it all cannot be missed.

Saint Alphonsus Liguori in "Conformity to God's Will," tells us, "Perfection is founded entirely on the love of God; Charity is the bond of perfection; and perfect love of God means the complete union of our will with God's."[5] He has thought of everything and has covered all the bases in giving us specific laws and rules to follow, all for our own happiness and safety. As a loving Father, he is instructing his children in a variety of ways, through Scripture, the Sacraments and our religious teachers. We have at our disposal all means necessary to reach our Heavenly destination.

The majesty of creation is a reflection of its divine architect, the Author of all goodness and beauty.

"All creatures bear a certain resemblance to God, most especially man, created in the image and likeness of God. The manifold perfections of creatures- their truth, their goodness, their beauty- all reflect the infinite perfection of God. From the greatness and beauty of created things comes a corresponding perception of their Creator."[6] The complex intricacy of creation is mirrored in the marvelous vision of the coherence of all created things.

> "Because God creates through wisdom His creation is ordered: "You have arranged all things by measure and number and weight."
> (Wisdom- 11:20)

> Indeed, even the very hairs of our head are all numbered.
> (Matthew- 10:30)

"Our human understanding, which shares in the light of the divine intellect, can understand what God tells us by means of His creation, though not without great effort and only in a spirit of humility and respect for the Creator and His work."

God is infinitely greater than all of His works: "You have set your glory above the heavens." Indeed, God's greatness is unsearchable. But because He is the free and sovereign Creator, the first cause of all that exists, God is present to His creatures' inmost being: "In Him we live and move and have our being." In the words of St. Augustine, God is "higher than my highest and more inward than my innermost self."[7]

It is clear that the nuns were dealing with some pretty hefty material in the deposit of faith that they were trying to impart on their little charges.

Chapter 6

"IMAGINARY LINES"
Our Reader Friends

The characters from the Scott Foresman and Company basal reader series were some of my best friends growing up. I couldn't wait to read about their latest escapades and pretend I lived in their perfect little world. They became so much a part of my thinking that I didn't even realize that I was learning to read. I loved John, Jean, Judy, Spot and Puff. I loved everything about their family and their lives, their house, their toys, their parents, and I loved how they treated one another. You never saw Father bombed and Mother never cursed at the kids. Spot never bit anyone and Puff never scratched anyone. Grandmother and Grandfather were always around doing something nice for someone. No Gambling Casinos for those two! They even had a Zeke, the handyman who worked around the house. I wanted to become an inhabitant of their wonderful little Reader world with white picket fences. I longed to journey through their sentimental little lives with them and have my own teddy bear called Tim and clown named Jack.

Sometimes if you pick up an old reader, the characters could have the wrong names. John was called Dick, Jean was known as Jane and Judy was named Sally. Who were these imposters? How could anyone make such a big mistake as to call our friends different names? "In 1941

Scott Foresman and Co. developed "The Cathedral Series" a special edition for Roman Catholic Schools which featured Catholic situations and changed the names of the characters to more Catholic names."[1] I will always remember them as John, Jean and Judy.

My favorite story was when the family was preparing for Jean's birthday. Father made her a big playhouse!!!! I had always wanted a playhouse ever since I read that story. Grandfather and the boys painted the house and Mother and Grandmother sewed little lace curtains for the windows!!! This was all stunning to me. To think that the whole family would work so hard so Jean could play, was mind boggling. There wasn't even a hint of sibling rivalry. John wasn't jealous and all bummed out because Jean was getting all the attention. There was no hitting, hair pulling or even a sneaky pinch.

Then the big day came and Grandmother and Grandfather drove the house over in their truck from the farm to give the gift to Jean! I was so happy for Jean! All I wanted to do was play with her in her new house.

As I grew older and became "too sophisticated," I guess I didn't need the little family anymore. I drifted away from them, but I will always be thankful for what I learned from my imaginary friends in their world of fantasy.

Eighty-five million little readers from 1930 until 1970 learned to See Spot Run! "The optimism and innocence portrayed within the covers of those books always evokes a warm nostalgic smile."[2] (I only had one Grandmother and she was busy praying the Rosary and going to bingo. I don't remember ever seeing her without a Rosary in her hand.) And if there were a bingo anywhere in the greater Philadelphia area, she would find it. With thirteen children and over seventy grandchildren, though, she wasn't about to start making curtains for anyone's playhouse. In

Shut Up and Get in Line

fact, I could just imagine her saying in her genuine Irish brogue, "Jeezus, Maredee and Jewsuf, have ya lost yer mind? Making caretons fir a dole hoose? I haven't even mate caretons fir me own hoose! I never knew my grandfather, yet I heard many wonderful stories about him and how he was very helpful to my Nanny and the children. I often wondered how a man with thirteen children could remain calm and sane. Then, one day I found the answer. I learned that my grandfather attended daily Mass at 6:00 A.M. before work. When I think of busy people like him who still manage to stay peaceful with all they have to do, I think they must have taken these words of St. Francis De Sales to heart; "Every day I spend an hour in prayer, except when I'm really busy- Then I spend two hours."[3]

Chapter 7

"FALL IN LINE"
We're Headed Home

The thinking and motivation behind the nuns' teaching styles came from a much higher power. To understand their desire to accurately pass things onto their students in the small world of their classrooms and their unyielding consistency when it came to order, discipline and doing things as perfectly as possible, we can look at the workings of the whole universe and see how it behaves.

"The universe obeys certain rules- laws to which all things must adhere. These laws are precise, and many of them are mathematical in nature. These laws are consistent with biblical creation. Everything in the universe, every plant and animal, every rock, every particle of matter or light wave, is bound by laws which it has no choice but to obey. The Bible tells us that there are laws of nature- "ordinances of heaven and earth." (Jeremiah 33:25) These laws describe the way God normally accomplishes His will in the universe. God's logic is built into the universe, and so the universe is not haphazard or arbitrary. It obeys laws of chemistry that are logically derived from the laws of physics, many of which can be logically derived from other laws of physics and laws of mathematics.

Shut Up and Get in Line

The most fundamental laws of nature exist only because God wills them to; they are the logical, orderly way that the Lord upholds and sustains the universe He has created. God does not change, and so He upholds the universe in a consistent, uniform way throughout time."[1]

(Jeremiah 33:25)

If the whole universe obeys God's laws, who are we not to follow them? God's creatures can be very obstinate and impatient. We all want to do things our own way. Forget the rules. We think we can do things better, faster or with less work involved, especially in our frenzied and decadent society. So what if we don't follow the Commandments. Who cares if we don't go to church? What does it matter if I cheat and lie? What business is it of yours if I go to pornographic movies? All of those things might be alright if it was your universe and you were making the rules. But the truth of the matter is that you are not the center of the universe. This is not your world and you do not make the rules. This is God's world and we are mere guests on this planet for a short time. It can be a very liberating feeling to realize that God is in complete control, and things will go much smoother for us when we do things His way. When we do the right thing, life becomes simple and we can bask in the peace and contentment knowing that there is a higher authority who is in charge of everything and watches over us constantly.

Thank God the Sisters, Priests and Teachers never gave up teaching us our faith and morals. Lessons we learned from them would serve us our whole lives. President Theodore Roosevelt warned us- "To educate a person in mind and not in morals is to educate a menace to society."[2]

How many of us were lost and returned to the church because we remembered something we learned in our youth or had a conversion of heart because of a distant memory of ourselves answering a catechism question or hearing a lovely hymn? How many of us were brought back to the faith of our fathers because of the beautiful prayers that we repeated daily as children? How many of us came full circle- sought the pleasures of the world, came up empty and returned to our precious roots?

With each step and each breath, we are drawing closer to our eternal home. "Physics, the most exact form of science tells us that all physical processes are part of a one-directional, essentially linear process. Scientists were not the first to perceive that such is the case. In a more commonsense form it was the Bible that first spelled out this unidirectional process of everything. First, there is creation, then cosmic and human history, all tending toward a final judgment and to a final consummation for all in heaven or hell."[3] Simply put, we're going home. We are headed home beginning with our birth and progressing daily toward our final destiny. One step at a time, we are inching closer to the Judgment Seat where we will stand alone before the Just Judge to give an accounting of our whole life.

"Mount Calvary is the academy of Love."
St. Francis de Sales

Chapter 8

"LINE OF SUCCESSION"
Double Duty Communion Dress

We finally reached the age of reason! We were seven now and our well informed consciences knew the difference between right and wrong, good and evil.

As we were being prepared to receive our first Holy Communion in second grade, our class was extremely excited. We knew that day would be the best day of our lives. The thought of receiving Jesus in the beautiful Sacrament of Holy Eucharist made us happy beyond words. When the nuns and teachers spoke of the Sacrament they beamed with joy and seemed ecstatic. We all loved hearing about Jesus and we knew we would be able to receive Him soon. We knew everything would be perfect on that day. Our souls would be completely pure and white because we were also receiving the Sacrament of Penance. The girls would wear beautiful white dresses, white veils, white shoes and white socks. Even the cruddiest of boys ended up looking respectable in their blue suits, white shirts and ties.

I was so happy when I went home to tell my mother that my big day was coming! She was thrilled and I knew she was glad to share my joy, but I never expected to hear the words she would utter. With a big grin on her face, she announced, "How wonderful! You will be wearing my wedding dress!" I thought I was hearing things, so I had her repeat it.

Again she said, "You're going to wear my wedding dress." She was still smiling ear to ear. I thought she had gone crazy.

NOOOOOOOOOO!!!!! I cried. Immediately, I began to sob as I pictured all my classmates in their little white dresses and me wearing a wedding gown with a long train. As if, I wanted to be a bride or something! How could she do this to me? "Stop your shenanigans," my mother warned, but the thought of me wearing that grown up dress was too much for me to bear. "I can't wear that wedding dress!" I protested. By this time, my sister, Rita heard the commotion and came in to see what was happening. I continued with my outrage. "I have to wear a wedding gown, Rita!" "No you don't, you Simpleton." She quickly clarified the situation. "Mom cut down her wedding gown to make a little dress. I had to wear it and so do you." I breathed a sigh of relief. Oh, that didn't sound so bad.

As it turned out, the dress was all satin and lace and very beautiful. I felt wonderful in the dress and I knew that my mother, my sister and I shared something special on our very special days.

> "Holy Communion is the shortest and safest way to heaven. There are others: innocence, but that is for little children; penance, but we are afraid of it; generous endurance for the trials of life, but when they come up we weep and ask to be spared. The surest, easiest, shortest way is the Eucharist."[1]
>
> Pope St. Pius X

Chapter 9

"IN LINE WITH HIS WILL"
Father Knows Best

The Divine Builder of the universe gave us specific instructions of how we are to conduct ourselves and exactly what we must do according to His perfect plan for us. Throughout Bible History, He was very precise with His directions. Notice His attention to detail in Genesis - "Build a boat for yourself out of good timber; make rooms in it and cover it with tar inside and out. Make it 450 feet long, 75 feet wide and 45 feet high. Make a roof for the boat and leave a space of 18 inches between the roof and the sides. Build it with three decks and put a door in the side."

Here's another example:

> Exodus 27: 1-8 "Make an altar out of acacia wood. It is to be square, 7½ feet long and 7½ feet wide, and it is to be 4½ feet high. Make projections at the top of the four corners. They are to form one piece with the altar, and the whole is to be covered with bronze. Make pans for the greasy ashes, and make shovels, bowls, hooks, and fire pans. All this equipment is to be made of bronze. Make a bronze grating and put four bronze carrying rings on its corners. Put the

grating under the rim of the altar, so that it reaches halfway up the altar. Make carrying poles of acacia wood, cover them with bronze and put them in the rings on each side of the altar when it is carried. Make the altar out of boards and leave it hollow, according to the plan that I showed you on the mountain."

Is there anything unclear in those directions? When God gives us His instructions, there is no question in what He means. From directing the building of Solomon's Temple to giving the Commandments to Moses, God's attention to specific details is very evident. Harmony reigns throughout the universe in God's unerring order. Because we are made in His image and likeness, we have a desire within us to also be ordered in our thinking and our actions. Chaos is rampant in the world when we are not replicating the ways and laws of the Heavenly Architect. I believe we have reached a critical stage in our country as we slide down the slippery slope of self-destruction. What went on in Sodom and Gomorrah that isn't going on every day in our country? And look what happened to them.

It's interesting how the churches were packed right after 9/11. There was standing room only! Why does it take a catastrophe or tragedy before we learn to do what we were told?

> "Obedience is the only virtue that implants the other virtues in the heart and preserves them after they have been so implanted."[1]
>
> Pope Saint Gregory the Great

Chapter 10

"CROSSING THE LINE"
The Bittersweet Chocolate Bunny

At Easter time in third grade, the school was having a fund raiser. You could order big chocolate bunnies or chocolate crosses to sell. I knew I wasn't allowed to go door to door to sell things to our neighbors. We didn't buy anything from them, and they didn't buy anything from us. This way, things would always be kept "even," and in my mother's wise words, "We wouldn't be beholden to anyone." I bemoaned my fate, "Why couldn't I order some? Everyone else was allowed."

The bunnies and crosses had all been ordered and I would not be participating. The day the bunnies and crosses arrived in the classroom was fun for my classmates and painful for me to watch. I thought, "If only I could get one of those bunnies, I would be the happiest girl on earth." I would take a chocolate cross too, even though they were smaller. Well, my bad luck was about to change. It was a miracle! Sister called Richard to pick up his two bunnies, but Richard said that he was only allowed to sell one. Sister said, "Who would like to sell the extra bunny?" Well, my hand shot up faster than my little heart was frantically beating. Poor Sister was about to make a huge mistake. "Catherine Moore," she called. As I giddily rushed up to her desk, she was saying something about having the money in by next week, but that part wasn't registering with me. Why didn't Sister know that you don't put two feet of rich milk chocolate in the grubby little hands of a skinny, hungry, sugar craven nine year old? So, he was mine now. I got him and I was on my way to the time of my life. I knew that the bunny would run into some foul play that day and would never make it to its intended destination.

When my bunny and I got off the bus, we headed for the field by my house where my friend Nancy and I would often kneel down and pray devoutly. (I prayed for a baby monkey and she prayed for a white stallion. We were sure that these two animals would one day be waiting in the field for us after school. We even thought it would be nice on the day that we first saw them, if the monkey was sitting on the back of the white stallion.)

As I sat down to feast, I had every intention of consuming the entire bunny. But, after I finished with the head, the ears, the candy eyes and part of the torso, I had put myself in a daze or some kind of sugar coma. The sight of me in that stupor could only be described as a big Baby Huey with a brown stained face, sticky fingers and a yucky gut load of goo. While I sat there in that state, reality was setting in, then the guilt. What had I done? Who would pay for this? I knew my parents couldn't. What would become of me now? I had broken all the rules. I betrayed everyone and I was only nine. As the sugar soared through my veins, I contemplated several scenarios that may help me work this out. I considered selling the remaining pieces of chocolate to my friends for a nickel a piece. Knowing that my mother had a sweet tooth, I thought for a fleeting moment that, perhaps I could win her compassion by enticing her with the chocolate.

Now I was experiencing something else that I had never planned on,

Shut Up and Get in Line

the worst bellyache of my life. Why, oh why did I do such a thing? (I guess I forgot to put on my thinking cap that day.) I was really regretting it now. To make matters worse, I decided to ignore the situation as long as possible. Maybe Sister won't ask me for the money next week and then no one will have to know. But, that wasn't to be. The following week when Sister was collecting for the candy, my worst fear came true. She remembered giving me the bunny and it was time for her to collect.

"Catherine Moore, come up." When Sister called my name to go to her desk, I felt like the Scarecrow in the Wizard of Oz with my shaky, rubbery legs that were carrying me to my just punishment. Sister sat there with her hand out looking at her paper, ready to check off my name. I stood there, loser that I was, regretting my sorry lot and wondering how a hunk of chocolate could make a person so ecstatically happy one week and so pathetically sad the next. Finally, Sister looked up from her paper and must have sensed the fear emanating from my skinny little body. Her eyes got big as she stared me down. "Where's your money?" "Well, I don't have it, Sister," I said sheepishly. "Where is it, Catherine?" "I wasn't allowed to sell the bunny, Sister." So, where is the bunny?" questioned Sister. I froze and just couldn't divulge my dirty, gluttonous little secret. Sister's tone was changing now as she insisted on knowing the whereabouts of the missing bunny. "CATHERINE, WHERE IS THE BUNNY?" I was on display in front of the class and I knew that an example would now be made of me that the students were not to forget. It seemed that one of the characteristics that all the nuns shared was the ability to use everything at their disposal to teach a lesson to the whole class. I was to be Sister's visual aid for this lesson and I knew from the dead silence that we had a captive audience. By now I had surmised that there was no way out. My cowardly ways were not serving me well. The truth would now be told. I mumbled something under my breath, but Sister couldn't hear me. "What did you say?" Sister demanded. I spoke again, this time just above a whisper. "I ate it." "What, I can't hear you," said Sister. I spoke louder. "I ate it." Sister shrieked. "Tell the class what you did, Catherine." I looked out at the sea of condemnation before me. "I ate it, class." The room was full of disapproving sounds. Some of them looked shocked and opened their mouths wide in disbelief. A few of them gasped, and the really mean, judgmental ones did that thing where you put your top teeth over your bottom lip, the thing that means, Shame on you.

Everyone knew how upset Sister was. She was now looking anxious and breathing heavily. After what seemed like an eternity, she said. "You will bring in the dollar that you owe us tomorrow!" After agreeing, I was free to return to the safety of my desk. Sister didn't miss a beat. "Take out your Spellers." With that, the whole class broke into song: S-P-E-L-L-I-N-G- Its spelling time, spelling time…etc. The song went to the tune of "Harrigan" I'll never forget that special song, because it took the attention off of me. I could breathe again for awhile at least until I got home and had to face the music there.

I waited until my mom was busy fixing supper before I said, "I need to bring in a dollar tomorrow." Her response was, "I told you before, we're not buying a pagan baby." I said, "It's not for that. I owe it to Sister and the class." Fast and furious, the questions shot out of my mother's mouth: "What? Did you break something? What in God's name did you do?" I hadn't realized that my big sister, Rita was listening from the other room. Rita was the perfect child, President of

Shut Up and Get in Line

her class and the smartest person I ever knew. She was also the only student I ever heard of that got a hundred on her report card! I answered my mother, "Well, Sister gave me a chocolate bunny and I knew I wasn't allowed to sell it, so…..I ate it." Rita raced in screaming, "You pig! She didn't even share it! Those rabbits are big too, Mom!" My mother could holler pretty good, so I knew what was coming. She had the same stunned look on her face that Sister had earlier. My sister joined the interrogation, "Where is it?" I confessed, "Upstairs in my drawer until yesterday when I finished it." Rita ran upstairs like a bat out of hell. My mom yelled, "What kind of a good Catholic girl would eat food that belongs to the Church? Just wait until your father gets home. You'll probably get the beating of your life with the big thick strap!" OH NO! I thought. Not the dreaded big thick strap! I heard about it now and then, but I never actually experienced it. I never even saw it or knew where it was kept. The tears began to flow. Meanwhile, Rita returned holding up the empty box that the bunny came in. "Look at this, Mom! Nothing left! Not one morsel!" Rita had all the flamboyance of a chief prosecutor. I wasn't paying too much attention to her and her physical evidence- the bunny box minus the bunny. All I could think about was the big thick strap. My tears and fears did not stop until my sympathetic father came home and assured me that he would pay my debt. He also added that I would not be going to the movies or roller skating for the next month. I felt lousy and turned to my big sister for consolation, but the sight of me made her sick. Scowling, she walked away declaring, "You made your bed, now lay in it, Thief."

All of this misery and grief for a few fleeting moments of guilty pleasure. Now I would be punished for an entire month. I had a few more bad days at school as a result of the bunny scandal, but things soon blew over and it would be someone else's turn to be the focus of the class' attention. All eyes would soon be off me and onto the three bad boys who were talkers. They had to wear red and white bows in their hair for their lack of self-control. Needless to say, I was very grateful for the bad boys and their big mouths.

Chapter 11

"WELCOMING LINE"
The Universal Church

I remember learning the four Marks of the Church in grade school; One, Holy, Catholic and Apostolic, but it wasn't until recently that I have experienced the true meaning of the word Catholic. Catholic or universal, means that our church welcomes all types. There is room at the Lord's table for everyone and everyone is encouraged to come- the poor and the rich, the young and the old, the infirmed, the prisoners, the lonely, the quiet and the shy, the joyful and effervescent, people from every profession, ethnicity, or walk of life. The Lord loves them all.

God in His Heaven must look down at His creation with great love and satisfaction. Just as a flower garden has many different colors, shapes and sizes, God's children too, are different colors, shapes and sizes. We all have our own special gifts and talents. A garden is spectacular to view because of the magnificent allure and the combination of all the flowers together. The garden would not be complete if the roses, the daffodils or the tulips were missing. For the garden to be perfect and breathtaking, all of the flowers must be present in all their beauty fulfilling the role for which they were created. So too it is with the children of God. I imagine that when He looks down at us, He feels great joy in seeing the beauty of each of His children fulfilling his or her destiny. Yet, how beautiful to see the big picture of all of us together. How special and unique each one of us is, and how He would miss even one who would go astray.

In conforming to God's laws, what role does joy and laughter play in our lives? There were many Saints and Jesus Himself, who commented about joy in Holy Scripture or the example they gave us in their own lives. Our Lord assured His Apostles, "Your joy no man shall take from you... Your joy shall be full."[1] Saint Thomas Aquinas said, "It is requisite for the relaxation of the mind that we make use from time to time of playful deeds and jokes."[2] Theophane Venard advises us-"Be merry, really merry. The life of a true Christian should be a perpetual jubilee, a prelude to the festivals of eternity."[3] The beloved St. Francis of Assisi says, "What are God's servants but His minstrels, who must inspire the hearts of men and stir them to spiritual joy!"[4]

When we surround ourselves with people of joy, it is contagious. We pick up on their positive outlook and invariably they give credit to the Lord as being the cause of their joy.

St. John Bosco often entertained the children with juggling, games and acrobatics, but he always prayed the Rosary with them first. He said, "If you don't pray for me, I may break my neck."[5]

St. Josemaria Escriva was a spiritual atomic bomb. "The first impression one gets from watching Escriva," John L. Allen Jr., Vatican Journalist writes after watching some films on the founder of Opus Dei in 2005, "is his effervescence, his keen sense of humor. He cracks jokes, makes faces, roams the stage and generally leaves his audience in stitches in off-the-cuff responses to questions from people in the crowd."[6] He was holy, yet joyful.

There are countless other joyful servants of the Lord. Pope John

Shut Up and Get in Line

Paul II, Saint Theresa, Padre Pio, Saint Thomas Aquinas, Blessed Giorgio Frassatti, to name a few. Saint Theresa of Avila prayed, "Lord, deliver me from gloomy saints."[7]

None of these people could contain his joy of the Lord. We all have the capacity for such joy if we surround ourselves with the love of Christ as Saint Patrick tells us; "Christ with me, Christ before me, Christ behind me, Christ within me, Christ below me, Christ above me, Christ at my right, Christ at my left, Christ in lying down, Christ in sitting, Christ in rising up, Christ in the heart of every man who thinks of me, Christ in the mouth of every man who speaks of me, Christ in every eye that sees me, Christ in every ear that hears me."[8]

Chapter 12

"THE BATTLE LINES ARE DRAWN"
No Dogs Allowed

Many of my classmates had pets and I would often get jealous of them when they used the names of their pets in spelling sentences. Our family never had any luck with pets.

Once we had a dog named Scotty, a cute scotch terrier. We could only admire his good looks from afar, because my dad tied him to the front doorknob and every time we walked by, Scotty would growl and try to bite us. Scotty was the last in a string of puppies that we would "try out" in my dad's words. Needless to say, Scotty did not work out and "had to go." There had also been a Blackie and a Frederick. Once these puppies became dogs, we got rid of them. They didn't work out. I also remember a little kitten named Velvet who I enjoyed very much, but once he became a cat, I never saw him again.

My desire to have my own baby monkey ended when I begged my dad for one. I told him I wanted to carry the monkey around like a baby and that it could even sit on my head or shoulder. My dad quickly replied, "Never! - You would have s_ _t running all down your back! They're not housebroken." Well, right then and there I was convinced. I never asked for a monkey again.

I watched "Lassie" on television every Sunday night. I loved Lassie

Shut Up and Get in Line

so much. I thought the coolest thing was when Lassie would jump through the window of Timmy's bedroom and come and go as she pleased.

I remember camping out in our backyard in a tent one summer night. All of the girls were sharing their dreams and fondest desires. When it was my turn, I said, "I really wish Lassie was mine. I love her so much. She could jump through my bedroom window and keep me company and protect me all night." I can still sense the innocence and candor in my voice and twinkle in my eye as I poured out the childish desires of my heart. My best friend, Babs, brought her big sister, Mary Ann to our camp out that night. Mary Ann was quick to comment about my wish. "Lassie would break her neck and it would be all your fault. Your bedroom's on the second floor, Dummy." Well, I don't know how I held back the tears. The thought of Lassie being hurt and me being responsible was too much to handle. The fact that I was a Dummy was humiliating, but since Mary Ann said it and Mary Ann was bigger and smarter than us, then it had to be true.

(Somewhere down the line I found out that there were four Lassies and felt violated beyond words.)

(Another camp-out that summer turned into a crying fest when we all learned that there was no Santa Claus. "Think about it," Mary Ann said, "What reindeer do you know that has a red light bulb nose?" Once Rudolph was thrown from the sleigh, Santa wasn't far behind.)

I'll never forget the day that Scotty had to go. My sister and I had just returned from the 9:00 Children's Mass. Our church sent around a bus on Sundays to pick up the children. My parents were heading out to the 11:00 Mass with little Jerry. Rita and I felt sorry for the poor little Scotty who was always tied up. So, we decided to give him a treat and see if we could get close enough to untie him. Our plan worked flawlessly. Rita distracted him with some sugar pops and she was able to set him free. We certainly did not expect Scotty's reaction to his newfound freedom. He tore off, almost knocking us over, and ran frantically through the whole house! He made dizzying circles around the living room and terrified us so much that we made a beeline for the kitchen table, the only place we felt safe. There we stood, two fearful and powerless sisters clinging to each other, held hostage by that tiny little cute dog. We thought he might have a little heart attack or pass out from exhaustion. An hour and a half later, we were rescued by our parents. We all agreed earnestly with my dad when he proudly proclaimed, "Do you see now why we had to keep him tied up?"

With the departure of Scotty came my dad's stern and steadfast promise, "We are NEVER getting another dog!" My mother backed him up wholeheartedly. We only cried for a little while after that warning. My dad was big at throwing out little nuggets of wisdom. (I think that's why I love quotations) When he saw the tears rolling down our cheeks, he sung out, "Time heals all wounds."

After awhile, he brought home a big turtle named Myrtle. My dad painted our phone number with white paint on Myrtle's shell. Sometimes, we would lose him, but after a few months, our next door neighbor would call and say that they spotted him on the way to their house.

I also remember a little round fish bowl with two goldfish swimming around and around. Turtles and fish just weren't the same as having a dog. I was sad because I knew I would never have a dog again. Over the years, I begged countless times, but the answer was always an emphatic NO.

Shut Up and Get in Line

One day when I was about fourteen, my mother was looking out the back window and made a big announcement. "Well, here comes our dog." Did I hear her right? What kind of a sick joke was this? There has to be some huge mistake! My eyes darted to my mother and I fixed my gaze on her. She went on, "Did you ever see such a beautiful sight as a boy and his dog?" I shot over to the window to see what was putting my mom in this euphoric state. Who do I see trudging through the field but my bratty little brother holding a puppy in his arms!! I knew this could never be! We were forbidden to have another dog. We all knew that. I begged for years, but to no avail! Well ain't this a crock? I couldn't see straight- "NO FAIR," I protested. "Me and Rita always wanted a dog, but we weren't allowed to have one!" My mom had a way of ignoring people that makes you think, "Am I really here and am I talking to myself?"

She ran to the door to welcome in the cute puppy and the dirty dog. I looked at my brother with such contempt. I closed my eyes into little slits and just stared at him. I was so busy protesting the unfairness of it all, that I never even looked at the adorable puppy in his arms. "Just wait until Rita hears about this!" As if Rita had any power to change the situation. I knew she would be equally shocked and appalled at this crummy turn of events. I continued, "When Rita gets home from work, she will not believe what is happening here!" (Rita had the best job in the world. She worked as a Candy Girl at the Towne Theatre) "Me and Rita were gypped!" My mom turned to me and said, "Really?" "Alright," I thought. "She's finally listening to me!" "Yeah," I complained, "Why should little Jerry get something that me and Rita were forbidden to have all of our lives?" My mom spoke, "I'm sorry you feel that way. Offer it up." Aw, she got me again. But why should

53

he be so happy when we weren't? Adding insult to injury, my brother announced, "This is MY dog." Now I really wanted to choke him. "Shut up, Jerry!" I warned. "Who died and left you boss?" Before long, though, I too fell in love with the little puppy. We named the dog Kelly and she was a dream dog. All of us were happy that this time we got a dog who "worked out."

(I still resented my little brother, though. I glared at him whenever I got the chance. I especially enjoyed it the day he tried to convince my dad that he should be in the Guinness Book of World Records for standing on one foot for four hours. My dad told him that it didn't count because he didn't have a witness. I just stood there gloating at him. I think my jealousy of him began soon after he was born. I realized that he was stealing my thunder. Today we're the best of friends. We love and encourage one another. I guess time does heal all wounds.)

Chapter 13

"LINE 'EM UP"
Family on Parade

Easter was always a huge production in our house and one of the biggest opportunities for strutting ourselves in all our Easter grandeur for the whole street to admire. My Mom would charge all of our outfits, so we would have new clothes, as she put it, "from the inside out." She did it up right, boy, and oh, what a spectacle we were! After we dressed in all our finery, Mom would send us down the driveway one at a time. We knew this was our time to shine, our big moment. First, little Jerry would be sent down. He was instructed to walk down the driveway slowly and go and stand up straight beside the car without leaning. When Jerry had done his part, it was my turn to go down in all my Easter splendor. I knew that the sight of me in my stunning attire, complete with white gloves, patent leather shoes and pocketbook, new Spring coat and Easter bonnet, would turn heads. I knew just how to play it up, pretending to be a model. I liked being on display and I knew I would make the family look good. Rita was next to show off in her beautiful outfit. I wanted to wear nylon stockings and heels like her, but I was too young until sixth grade. Then I was allowed to wear stockings and French Heels. By eighth grade I had graduated into the Queen Ann heel which was about a quarter inch higher than the French heel, but nowhere near the size of "the mother of all heels," the spike heels which my mom wore. How those pointy high heeled shoes didn't cripple her, I will never know.

She glided down the (runway) driveway in her splendid, huge, royal blue lace hat, her dress with big royal blue flowers, white gloves, big sparkling jewelry and purse. Once she reached the car, it was now time for my dad to come down with the camera, take pictures, and tell my mom that she looked liked The Cat's Meow. Now for the really interesting part; after we had all done our bit and paraded down to the car, my mom sent us back to do it all again! I guess the neighbors who missed the first show, would be able to catch the second one.

After church, we always went to the Levittown Easter Parade where we could really show off. Of course, we wanted to win the contest as the "Best Dressed Family," but the families with the cute babies always won. Some of them even had big decorated coaches. Every year when we saw the cute babies all dolled up, we knew we didn't stand a chance. I didn't care though. I knew I had a box of real live colored chicks waiting to play with me at home.

I never liked the judges. What were they writing down when they looked at us, and what were their qualifications for judging us? Anyway, my dad said the whole thing "was fixed."

By the time we were nearing the teenage years, my mom finally gave up on the Easter Parade. She knew we wouldn't smile for the judges anymore. When they looked us over, we just shot them a look of boredom or disgust.

Even though we didn't win a prize in the Easter Parade, we were always big winners with our Easter chicks. They loved to see us coming. They ran all around and were a beautiful sight to behold, green ones, purple ones, hot pink - every color of the rainbow. We always played with our chicks a good two weeks after Easter, but then they had to go.

Chapter 14

"CRYSTALLINE MEMORIES"
Christmas Joy

Annually on Christmas Eve, all the neighborhood kids and even some adults, went around the street singing Christmas carols. We especially liked the snowy Christmas Eves and the warm feeling of spreading to others all the happiness and love in our hearts. I even liked going to school during Advent when we were being prepared for the great event that we would soon be celebrating.

Every year, the day before Christmas vacation, our Pastor sent a box of candy over to the school for each boy and girl. Then we exchanged Pollyannas and would get to watch "The Spirit of Christmas," a Bell Telephone Puppet Show of "The Night Before Christmas" and "The Nativity Story." Each year as they rolled in the big projector, all the kids were beside themselves with joy. When we reached the upper grades, there were comments made about how we were ripped off because we could see all the puppet strings. (But secretly we still enjoyed watching.) Our Sisters and Teachers would remind us to do good deeds. They said that each good deed that we did would add another piece of straw to the nice cozy bed for our Lord and it would be all ready for Him by Christmas morning. The beautiful way they described how warm and inviting we should make the safe little room in our hearts for Jesus, is something that has stayed with me my whole life. There was something

Shut Up and Get in Line

so special and inspiring about going to Mass on Christmas Day. The sight of the big Manger scene and the choir singing Christmas hymns as we celebrated Mass together was too beautiful and amazing to put into words.

The first glimpse of our Christmas tree with the presents under it was always magical. The memory of my favorite Christmas has been etched in my mind since I was eight years old. It is as crystal clear to me now as if it happened yesterday. My sister and I awoke just before dawn. The scene had already been set and waiting for us. The beauty of the Christmas tree with the colored lights, tinsel, and bubble bulbs was spectacular. The Nativity Scene reflected the tree lights and glowed in the dark. Strands of silvery tinsel shimmered in a quiet dance with the lights. The room was bathed in a mesmerizing kaleidoscope of color. The trains were sitting there waiting to be turned on and there was complete silence. There was sheer beauty in the still silence of that setting. We were frozen for a moment and just stared at the scene, too perfect to disturb. Then something caught my eye in the corner of the room. It was a big store complete with boxes of little food! I rushed to go behind the window of the store. My heart was racing. How happy I was to discover the tag on it had my name! My own store! What a dream come true! In that moment, everything else disappeared. Then I saw my other gifts- a little table that had been set with dishes, utensils, a coffee pot set, orange juice glasses and little toaster! Was I dreaming? I noticed that sitting at the table was a beautiful Ballerina Doll. The sight took my breath away. This was the closest I had ever come to ecstasy. My wonderful gifts! What a lucky girl I was. Meanwhile, little Jerry was sitting in some kind of push car heading for the trains and my sister was in her own little world across the room. She was playing records on a big juke box with flashing colored lights that said "Junior Juke." This was high tech for 1959! Between the big cardboard store and Junior Juke, our house became an attraction for all the neighborhood kids. We played for years with that store, using it for puppet shows, lemonade stands, carnival booths, backyard shows, even as a grocery store. My cousin Terri still comments to this day that the store was the best thing that ever happened to us. I think our favorite use of the store was when we pretended it was a TV and my sister, cousins and I acted out episodes from "The Twilight Zone."

(Junior Juke would become special to me also. A few months later on my birthday, my mom was hearing me a long Catechism question while my sister was lurking in the background. When I memorized the answer perfectly, I heard a new record playing on Junior Juke. It was called "Tan Shoes with Pink Shoe Laces." I jumped for joy to have my very own 45 RPM record. I was really somebody now!)

The memory of that Christmas always brings a smile to my face. Now, I think how blessed we were to be given such beautiful memories and special times in our lives. I like to picture our dear Lord smiling down at all His children playing and enjoying their youth. The sweet innocence of childhood is so fleeting and yet so miraculous. Growing up in the fifties and sixties was a special time I will never forget. My mind often flashes back to fond memories of those bygone days, the charming innocence of youth, and the sweet world we knew.

Shut Up and Get in Line

"THE SWEET WORLD WE KNEW"

We ate Corn Pops, Frosted Flakes, Maypo and Trix,
They gave us our breakfast sugar fix.

We drank our Bosco, Kool-Aid or Tang,
Then ran outside to play with the gang.

We played Hula Hoops, Marbles, Dodge Ball and Jacks,
Wearing big red lips that were made of wax.

We had metal Slinkys and Comic Books
And Dinner Dish sets for little girl cooks.

Wonder Bread, Skippy and Jelly for lunch
With Scooter Pies, milk or Hawaiian Punch.

Then out again to have some fun
With our Old Maid Cards or Water Gun.

We hugged Raggedy Ann and dried Tiny Tears eyes,
Patty Play Pal was bigger than most of the guys.

We jumped on our Pogo Sticks, rode our new Schwinn,
Raced fast in our Converse hoping to win.

The Good Humor Man came at two o'clock
With ice cream for every kid on the block.

A dime got you a Rocket or Push-Up Pop.
Fudgcicle, or Drumstick with nuts on the top.

Cowboys and Indians hid in the trees,
And Superman's cape swung in the breeze.

Our Radio Flyers always were there
To pull our friends and our toys anywhere.

At snack time we shared more sugary treats,
Good 'N Plenty, Pez and all kinds of sweets.

Marshmallow Cones, Chunky's and Hershey Bars,
Tootsie Rolls, Candy Buttons, Snowballs and Mars.

We liked Turkish Taffy, but even one piece
Could pull the fillings right out of our teeth.

We swam and camped or fished for days
And went to the Drive-Ins in our PJ's.

We got dirty and scraped all week as we'd play
But squeaky clean for Church on the Lord's Day.

We dined on T.V. Dinners and pot pies,
McDonald's fifteen-cent burgers and ten cent French fries.

Making "Pizza from a Box" with Chef Boyardee
Was always a suppertime sight to see.

We dove under our school desks and were told to stay calm,
So we would survive being hit by The Bomb.

Our coonskin hats hung near our beds,
Some kids had arrows right through their heads!

Toni Home Perms didn't turn out very well,
Most of the girls had hair like Clarabell.

Shut Up and Get in Line

Snowee's arrival would sound with a Beep
And onto his truck all the children would leap.

There were Juicy Fruits and Soda Bottles of wax,
Candy Necklaces, Snow cones and Cracker Jacks.

Raisinettes, Milk Duds and Carmel Creams
And everything else in a kid's wildest dreams.

We jumped on our bikes at the end of the day
And followed the trucks with the pesticide spray.

Then nylons, transistors and forty-fives
Would one day replace the toys in our lives.

There would be no more Red Rover or Mr. Machine,
With Candy Cigarettes we could not be seen.

Match Box-Cars and Trains have come to a stop
And the beads on our necks will nevermore pop.

Now, faceless sits Mister Potato Head,
Our Nancy Drew books no longer are read.

No more cap guns, snow days or "egg in a cup,"
Walky-Talkies are silent; Chatty Cathy shut up.

G.I. Joes and Frisbees now collect dust
While our Skates and Scooters have started to rust.

Our swings are empty, "Paint by Numbers" are faded,
Nevermore will our baseball cards be traded.

The world is awaiting, our play is now done,
Ready or not, here we come!

Farewell Tinker Toys and beloved basketballs,
We must leave you behind when Destiny calls.

Our innocent youth will forever be gone,
We would love to stay but time marches on.

So long Carefree Days and Childhood Joys-
Goodbye to those dear little girls and boys.

With the sweet world of yesteryear each one must part,
But hopes to stay always a child at heart.

Chapter 15

"A LONG LINE OF RELATIVES"
Our Family Album

Our family albums are visual records of the milestones in our lives. When we look through the photo album of any Catholic family, a fascinating and beautiful reality comes to light. All of the important family pictures are centered around the Sacraments, the Church Feast Days and the Liturgical Year. Our faith unfolds before our very eyes. Baptisms, First Holy Communion Days, Confirmation pictures, Weddings, Christmas, Easter. Take away the faith related pictures and what is left? Not much.

As you open the book, you see pictures of the new baby on his birthday. He is immediately named for a Saint that will become one of his patrons and special intercessors. Pictures of his Baptism grace the pages depicting the little one and his relatives as he is welcomed into his new church family. He becomes truly pure and grace-filled as the cleansing water of Baptism is poured over him and the sin he inherited from his first parents is washed away. What a perfect and beneficent plan was put forth by our Creator! He provided for our Redemption through the merits of His Son, our loving Savior, Jesus Christ.

As children of God and members of the Communion of Saints, (the Church Triumphant in Heaven, the Church Suffering in Purgatory, and the Church Militant on earth), we have a rich family history which includes many colorful personalities from our lineage.

"From one man He created all races of mankind and made them live throughout the whole earth. He Himself fixed beforehand the exact times and limits of the places where they would live. He did this so that they would look for Him, and perhaps find Him as they felt around for Him. Yet God is actually not far from any one of us; as someone has said, 'In Him we live and move and exist.' It is as some of your poets have said, 'We too are His children.' Acts-17:26-28

We are reminded of our long ancestral lineage from the first man and woman ever created. We can picture all those who came after Adam and Eve and the good old gang, Cain and Abel, Abraham, Isaac and David and all the way down the line to Mary, Joseph and Jesus.

If our family albums were complete, and we were able to include pictures of all of our ancestors, we could see more clearly how we are all related and how intertwined our lives really are. Wouldn't it be interesting to see the resemblances and family traits (both positive and negative) which were passed down to us?

Perhaps we should leave a space in our albums to remember some of those who went before us and the tremendous impact which they had on our lives.

> "In the Scriptures, our people are shown to be made one; so that just as many grains collected into one and ground and mingled together make one loaf, so in Christ, who is the heavenly Bread, we know there is one body, in which our whole company is joined and united."
>
> Hilary of Poitiers

Chapter 16

"GOD WRITES STRAIGHT WITH OUR CROOKED LINES"
Some Family Nostalgia

We had some real characters in our family line, didn't we? Let's begin with Adam and Eve. We all agree that we were off to a rough start having those two as our parents. It seems that no one can wait to see Adam and Eve to give them a piece of our minds. We're just like all ungrateful children who blame their parents for everything that ever went wrong in their lives! "It's all your fault because you spoiled me," or "It's all your fault because I didn't get something I needed when I was young." But, wait a minute! What did Adam and Eve do that we didn't do or wouldn't have done? We were also disobedient. We were given the Commandments and we broke them over and over again. In our haste to judge others, we are missing the big picture which shows our own sins and shortcomings.

We could also see our brothers, Cain and Abel in our albums. We can quickly recognize the sibling rivalry, envy and anger that was passed on from them.

We remember the bravery of our brothers Daniel and David. When we think of the enormous faith and courage of Daniel in the lion's den and David fighting a giant, we wonder if we have inherited any of their heroic traits. "Yet David, the greatest King of Israel, showed his human flaws committing adultery with Bathsheba and then having her husband, Uriah killed. (2 Sm11). But, when David repented, God fulfilled the promise to establish David's throne forever.

Sometimes, we feel like our little brother, Zaccheus (Lk 19:1-10)-: too small to see what is going on, too short to catch the great events passing by, much less able to do anything to change them. Yet the message of Zaccheus tells us that we- little, flawed, small in stature, weak in power- can still be used by God in His divine plan.

There is an old saying to the effect that "God writes straight with crooked lines." The divine plan for salvation is a straight, unchanging line leading us, through Christ, to perfection with God. But God, in infinite and unfathomable wisdom, brings about that perfect salvation through very imperfect means; us. As sacramental theologian Father Nicholas Halligan, OP, said, "The Father begins the work of salvation in us and brings it to perfection. If we do anything, it is only because He does it in us." Through the events of salvation history, we see God at work, writing salvation's story through the crooked line of human history.

Genesis 21 tells us that Abraham, our Father in faith was one hundred years old, And Sarah, ninety (Gn18), when their only son Isaac was born. Both were old and frail, well past their productive ages. Yet, as pointed out in Heb.6:11. "There came forth from one man, himself as good as dead, descendants as numerous as the stars in the sky and as countless as the sands on the seashore."

Jacob, father of the tribes of Israel, did not start well in life. He stole his brother's birthright (Gn27) and then ran off with his father-in-law's family and goods (Gn 30 and 31). "But, in the end, Jacob mended relations with both Laban and Esau, even risking his life by facing his brother alone." (Gn33)[1]

These people were our ancestors. "And don't forget the women in our family tree: Tamar, who tricked Judah into fathering her twin sons; Rahab, the harlot, who saved Joshua's spies in the conquest of Jericho" (Jos2:1-18). Even Sarah laughed when God promised her a son (Gn18-12).

Then there were Jesus' followers. They found many crooked lines in their lives, too. Peter, big and good-hearted, sometimes at a loss for words, other times, saying just the wrong thing. (Remember, "Get behind me Satan?). He even denied Jesus three times on that fateful night. But Peter ran to the tomb to learn the unimaginable truth and then -three times- declared his love for Christ.

Paul (still called Saul), on fire for his faith, "persecuted the Church of God violently and tried to destroy it." (Gal 1:11). He had to be struck blind before he saw salvation's straight lines. But then to him, "the very least of all holy ones, this grace was given, to preach to the Gentiles the inscrutable riches of Christ." (Eph 3:8)

And lest we think God's chosen ones, the crooked lines with which he writes straightly, have it easy even as they follow God's will, recall Paul's words to the Corinthians: "a thorn in the flesh was given to me… Three times I begged the Lord about this that it might leave me, but he said to me, "My grace is sufficient for you, for power is made perfect in weakness." (2 Cor 12:7-9)

Divine power is made perfect in weakness. Crooked lines are made straight. A chief tax collector, the most despised of "governmental thieves," vows to give back anything he has wrongfully taken and more. And what happens? "Today, salvation has come to this house… for the

Son of Man has come to seek and to save what was lost."[2]

Can we see ourselves in the good old gang?

"Are we small like Zaccheus? Proud like Paul? Weak like David? Frail like Abraham? Old like Sarah? Doubting like Thomas?

Each of us has crooked lines. Zaccheus teaches us that crooked lines can be made straight. All we must do is be willing to offer ourselves to God's hand.

As Pope John Paul II said in a homily on Zaccheus: "Thanks to the closeness of Jesus, of His words and His teaching, this man's heart begins to be transformed… This opening of the heart in the encounter with Christ is a pledge of salvation." And just as He once did with Zaccheus, so at this moment Christ stands before the men and women of our age. He seems to say to each person individually; "I must stay at your house today." (June 9, 1999).

Zaccheus, a little man, despised by others, faced the enormity of all salvation offered to him. Overjoyed, he climbed down from his crooked tree limb and came straight home to salvation."[3]

Our relatives had many imperfections as do we, but through the splendorous mercy and benevolence of our Lord, He loves each of us nonetheless, whether crooked or straight. We are all endowed with special talents and gifts unique to ourselves and must strive to fulfill the mission to which each was entrusted here on earth. Imbued with every spiritual gift from our Creator, we can successfully reach our destination and fall in line in the special spot that has been reserved for us throughout salvation history.

Are we ready for Jesus to stay at our house? Are our souls pure and swept clean of any trace or stench of sin? Are there cobwebs or residual hidden shame of a guilty conscience? Are we clinging to an offense that repeats itself and tries to stick to the innermost walls of our souls? Do we feel as though we are being held in bondage by some past indiscretion? When Jesus says He must stay at our house today, we must be ready. Welcome Him into a beautiful and peaceful abode fragrant with the essence of prayer and good deeds. Invite Him to rest His precious Head in a pristine and comforting environment overflowing with gratitude and praise. Once He brings His bountiful blessings of goodness and light to your house, He will fill it with His Divine love, glorious presence, and peace beyond all reason. Remain in His wondrous love, and when Jesus comes to your house, cling to Him and never let Him go.

FAMILY SECRETS

Everyone had secrets, but paradoxically in Levittown, no one had secrets. The homes were so close and there were so many kids, that as soon as you told someone your secret, the whole neighborhood knew. Plus, it was said that the Milkman, the Breadman and especially the Mailman, "had the goods on everyone."

Any number of fathers could have had the distinction of being "the town drunk." The only reason Timmy's dad won the title is because Timmy's folks took their battles outside. Poor Timmy never knew when the afternoon school bus turned the bend, if he was going to see his parents rolling around on the grass sluggin' it out. It was often up to Timmy and his siblings to jump in and break it up before they went down for the count.

Then the children would restore peace and lead the soused pair back in the house.

"Love is patient, love is kind, love never ends."[1]
Corinthians 13:4-8

Shut Up and Get in Line

I loved jumping out from hiding places and scaring people, especially my sister, Rita. I was shaping up to be an unsuitable companion for her. So, she got herself a new friend named Bejjil. Bejjil was an imaginary friend, so this secret "just couldn't get out!"

How's that for a kick in the teeth? Rita preferred the company of some kid who didn't exist, over my company! (Oh crumb, what does that say about me?) My parents were horrified when Rita pretended to play with Bejjil and they laid something heavy on me. As our little trio huddled, they whispered, "Maybe if this one plays with Rita all day, she won't have any time for Bejjil." It seemed that it would be through my efforts that Bejjil would be killed off. Now I had to compete with an enemy that I couldn't see! I'd jump out and scare her to death if I knew where she was. What if she runs faster or plays nicer than me? Hey, what if the S.O.B. is bad-mouthing me behind my back? Bejjil was a sneaky thing and I hated her guts. I'll show her! I'll be a better friend to Rita and not pop out and scare her anymore! So, amidst all the family paranoia, Bejjil left as quietly as she came and the family secret never got out.

Chapter 17

"GOD'S PLUMB LINE"
The Church

Our most wonderful relative by far was Jesus of Nazareth. The traits which He passed on to us were all good ones, Faith, Hope, Love, Joy, Peace, Patience, Goodness. Because He was God made man, we were given supernatural gifts from Him. He even told us that He would never leave us orphans. He left us His Holy Spirit and His very own Body and Blood. This is the miraculous truth of our interconnectedness. Through the cleansing waters of Baptism, we enter into His family as His adopted sons and daughters and through the reception of the Blessed Sacrament, we join in the Sacred mystery and beautiful reality that we all have His Body and Blood coursing through our veins. The image of the Communion Line is the most wonderful family picture we could ever put into the album. The sight of our brothers and sisters receiving the Sacrament and sharing the Eucharistic meal together is a joy to behold.

Saint John of Damascus instructed us, "The teaching of the Church is both the starting line and the finish line for the race; it is the bridle of a tightly reined horse."[1]

Jesus left us a Church to teach, to sanctify and to rule. We are secure in the comforting arms of Holy Mother Church, our safe haven, and our home away from home. The Church guides and protects us all as members of the household of God- Eph. 2:1-9

Our filial ties are rooted in Christ Jesus and the Holy Catholic Church. Our family business centers on discipleship and the spreading of truth and love to all those we meet. We can set a good example to others by demonstrating strong family values and never dragging our good name through the mud. Our familial love should be extended to all and apparent in our demeanor and our actions. -"They'll know we are Christians by our love."

We should reach out to everyone regardless of their imperfections, addictions, or prejudices. Our genealogy has been passed down, positive and negative traits, dysfunctions and goodness, sinfulness and saintliness. It's all in the family.

Just as lines continue infinitely, so too do our souls. There will be no end to the blissful splendor of Heaven or the sorrowful doom of Hell. 2Esdras:27-38 tells us, "Then God Most High will say to the nations that have been raised from the dead, 'Look! I am the One whom you have denied and refused to serve; it is My commands that you have rejected. Look around you; there is joy and peace in one direction, fire and torment in the other. That's what He will say to them on Judgment Day." How blessed we will be if we remain loyal to our Lord and His worldwide family, the Universal Church, until that glorious day when we have all reached our Heavenly Homeland.

We will have the most awesome and unimaginable family reunion with all of our relatives, and celebrate in the company of the most perfect and beloved Divine Family, the Father, the Son and the Holy Spirit. There a banquet has been set for all the faithful to enjoy a glorious eternity.

"Against Christ's army the world arrays a twofold battle line. It offers temptation to lead us astray; it strikes terror into us to break our spirit. At both of these approaches, Christ rushes to our aid, and the Christian is not conquered."

St. Augustine

Chapter 18

"SAFETY LINE"
Family Loyalty

We must protect our great heritage and precious family lineage. It is essential to educate ourselves and learn all we can about our beautiful faith. We need to help others draw closer to the Lord and we must be capable of answering their difficult questions. It is a joy to read and learn from the Bible, the love letter from our homeland written to us by our Heavenly Father. Another outstanding habit to form is the reading of spiritual books and becoming proficient in the Catechism, just as we were as children learning from the nuns. They made sure that we knew it and they drilled us over and over until they knew we understood it. As Catholics, we know more than we think we do about the Bible from listening to the readings at Mass. These readings have been repeated for us throughout the years during every Mass we have ever attended. We also need the strength and constancy of the Sacraments and prayer. It is our duty to know that Apostolic Authority was handed down from Jesus to the first Pope, Peter, and to all of his successors. Sure, we probably had a few characters in the line of our Popes. Popes are human too, but we can be sure that any teaching they did on faith and morals was infallible.

The Church has been attacked by the uninformed, the misguided and evildoers from within and without, for two thousand years, but it will stand until the end of time. Even so, it is our responsibility to protect and defend our historical relatives and the legacy of Holy Mother Church. When we are educated and know all the facts, events and people who played major roles in Bible History, our history, our legacy, we will easily be able to counter. Anytime a ridiculous or outlandish story pops up from even an unlikely source as little Opey from Mayberry, who decided that Jesus had a wife and it was Mary Magdalene and the two of them had children, we will easily laugh off these outrageous insults against the Church. (Gee-Aunt Bea would have been broken-hearted and Andy would have washed his blasphemous little mouth out with soap.) This is Revisionist History and an attempt to shatter the very core of Christianity by attacking the divinity of Our Lord and the truths of Sacred Scripture. Some writers are using fragments of the inspired writings of the Holy Bible and mixing in fictional and fabricated inventions of their own imaginations. Their twisted ideas confuse those without a solid foundation in Church teaching and they may even buy into these distorted works of fantasy. We need to learn our faith and read the Bible every day. Then, when we hear an uninformed or false statement, we will intelligently and instinctively know the true facts and respond accordingly.

It's interesting that the only people who leave the church are the ones who do not know and study their faith. They would never leave it, if they realized Who they are leaving behind. Even more fascinating is the fact that the great surge of those coming into the faith are Protestant ministers and those who study, research and discover the Truth.

The former Protestant minister, Scott Hahn, tells how -"out of consuming curiosity, I went to Mass one day. I sat there looking at all these people. I looked at their devotion, their sincerity taking time out in the middle of the day to worship; and I watched how, during the Consecration, their heads were lowered, their lips were moving, their hearts were stirring. I went back the next day, and the next and the next. Within a week or two I had fallen head over heels in love with the Mass. I was transformed. The Eucharist became, in a sense, the all-controlling central desire of my life! I can't describe to you the passionate thirst and hunger that came over me day after day as I saw all of these people going up and being fed with the Body and Blood of our Lord!"[1]

Father Coropi observed that there are so many different denominations and he respects them all, but Christ wants one flock. It's amazing how some people try out different churches, as if they are picking out a candy bar. If they don't "feel good" there, they just try another one. They want fellowship and "big feel good" concerts. When you go into some churches, everyone's having a grand old time socializing. It's astounding when you hear someone say, "We're looking for a new church." Well- gee, how about trying the old one, the oldest one- really trying it, learning about it and practicing what it teaches? If it's fellowship you crave, why fellowship with God's creatures, when you can fellowship with God, Himself in the Holy Eucharist? So, don't exchange "fellowship with man and a few laughs," for the Lord, Himself- Body, Blood, Soul and Divinity. Return to the church which Jesus left to Peter. It was only to Peter that the keys to the church were given when Jesus said, "Thou art Peter, and upon this rock I will build my church."

In his great wisdom, Saint Cyprian of Carthage tells us; "His Church is one, His see is one, founded by the voice of the Lord on Peter. No other altar can be set up, no other priesthood instituted apart from that one altar and that one priesthood. Whoever gathers elsewhere, scatters."

As sons and daughters of our Heavenly Father, we are members of the household of God. Eph.2-19. As heirs to Heaven we have a huge family responsibility. We must be committed to protecting our good name. With the perfect example of family loyalty given to us by the Holy Family, Jesus, Mary and Joseph, we too must learn to stick together, promote unity and never waver in our defense of the truth.

> "The Church has ever proved indestructible. Her persecutors have failed to destroy her, in fact it was during times of persecution that the Church grew more and more; while the persecutors themselves, and those whom the Church would destroy, are the very ones who came to nothing… Again, errors have assailed her, but in fact, the greater the number of errors that have arisen, the more has the truth been made manifest… Nor has the Church failed before the assaults of demons: for she is like a tower of refuge to all who fight against the Devil."[2]
>
> Saint Thomas Aquinas

Chapter 19

"IN THE LINE OF FIRE"
Hand-Me-Down Confirmation Name

Third graders in our school received the Sacrament of Confirmation. Sister Veronice, our teacher, spoke beautifully about the Sacrament and we couldn't wait until our Confirmation Day. She told us that we were already Soldiers in the Army of Christ because we had received Baptism, Penance and Holy Eucharist, but now the Holy Spirit is coming to give us special gifts that we would need for our life journey. Sister said that the gifts we were getting were; Wisdom, Understanding, Knowledge, Counsel, Fortitude, Piety and Fear of the Lord. We were elated that we would be getting these new gifts and we knew that we would be wonderful people for life. Sister then sweetened the pot. Not only would we be getting these seven gifts from the Holy Spirit, He will also be giving us twelve fruits. We all looked at one another in confusion; as if some fruit delivery man would be arriving in our classroom. Then Sister explained that the fruits we would be getting are spiritual fruits; Charity, Joy, Peace, Patience, Benignity, Goodness, Long Suffering, Mildness, Faith, Modesty, Continency and Chastity. She also told us that the Bishop would be coming to give us a new name that we could pick out ourselves! I already had two names- Catherine and Mary and I was thrilled that I was going to get to pick a new one too. What could be better? I'm going to get all these new gifts and fruits from the Holy Spirit and a new name to boot. Sister gave us a special card for our parents to fill out with the name of our Sponsor and our Confirmation name. She told us to read about the Saints we chose, and learn who they were and what they did. I had a few good names in mind.

I ran home from the bus to tell my mom the great news. "Mom, I'm going to receive the Sacrament of Confirmation and I get to pick a new name!" She was busy folding laundry, but she said, "Elizabeth." "What?" I responded. "Elizabeth, that's your name." "No," I objected. "Sister said I get to pick it out and…" I sensed things were not going right and the tears were about to fall. My mom interrupted me. "Elizabeth is my name, and it's going to be yours too." (She wasn't budging) By this time I was fully sobbing and in between my breaths, I said, "But I don't like that name." My sister had entered the scene now and was watching the action. "I want the name Theresa," I said.

"No," my mom nixed it. "That name's taken." What? I thought, "How could that be?"

"What do you mean taken?" "Your cousin has that name already." "But," I protested, "That's Terri's first name, that won't matter." My mom asked me, "Do you want to be a copycat?"

"Well," I questioned her, "How about Ann? She was the Grandmother of Jesus!" My sister, Rita, was quick to add her two cents. "Well, let's see," she said. "You already have Catherine Mary and Ann would make it MaryAnn. Do you want to become like MaryAnn Bader?" "NO!" I shot back. (We all knew that MaryAnn was the bad kid on the street.) My mother repeated, "Elizabeth is her name. If it's good enough for Elizabeth Taylor, it's good enough for us." I said, "I hate that name!" "What?" scolded my mother. "Can it! Do you want the

Shut Up and Get in Line

Blessed Mother to hear you? Do you want her to know that you don't like her cousin's name?" Oh, no, what had I done? I didn't want to hurt Mary or Elizabeth. "What do you say?" my mom asked. I said apologetically, "I'm sorry, I'll take Elizabeth." On the way out of the room, my sister gave me a look of disgust and warned me, "Oh, yeah? Well you just better say you're sorry to those two."

> "To each who receives the Spirit, it is as if he alone received Him; yet the grace the Spirit pours out is quite sufficient for the whole of man-kind."[1]
>
> Saint Basil the Great

Chapter 20

"SCARY MOVIE LINES"
Hansel and Gretel

Between the air raid drills, trying to memorize the state capitals and Arithmetic drill and mental, we were pretty much walking on eggshells. We longed for the weekend when we usually found refuge at the afternoon matinee at a local movie theatre or the Rollerama Skating Rink. Back then, going to the movies was a real event. Besides the double feature, there were cartoons, newsreels depicting current events and the lifestyle and gossip of the famous people of the day, coming attractions, car races, horse races and human races! Also lots of advertisements for the concession stand starring the dancing and singing popcorn boxes and soda bottles. A man came on the stage before the movie to get the pint-sized audience all pumped up about the prizes to be won if your car, horse, or man won the race!

The problem with going to the movies is that it usually involved some kind of trauma from the latest fairy tale on the big screen. Invariably the movie would involve a witch or some sinister character who always managed to remain in our psyches to torment us at night.

Of all the children's movies I saw, I was most freaked out by the terrifying tale of Hansel and Gretel. It was my first experience with evil. When I first learned that those two unfortunate siblings were kicked out

Shut Up and Get in Line

of their house and turned into the woods, I was horrified. Whaaaaat? Did rotten, no-good, monstrous people like that wicked step-mother really exist? Why would anyone want to hurt two good little children, especially children who had no mother? First of all, how could a father ever send his children away? I was absolutely crushed! I walked every painful step with the unfortunate pair and then, suddenly, I felt sheer bliss at the sight of the spectacular candy gingerbread house! My heart raced as they would finally find true happiness in this sweet haven of love and sugary delight! How blessed they were. I couldn't imagine two luckier kids. What could possibly be better than this? But, then the unspeakable! A wretched witch put Hansel in a cage to fatten him up so she could cook and eat him!!!!! Whoa!! No Way!!! Well, my heart sank and my soul was seared to the very core. The wailing that went on with that young audience was pathetic. Most kids covered their eyes. I had enough of this disturbed bunch and wanted to run screaming from the theatre! Nothing in my life thus far had prepared me for the possibility of such evil existing in the world. No other witch had affected me like the Hansel and Gretel witch, though the Wizard of Oz witch came pretty close.

We all literally jumped for joy when Gretel pushed the witch into the oven. It seemed the whole theatre shook in cheerful celebration! I remember admiring Gretel's courage and quick thinking. Still, the peril of it all took its toll on our youthful innocence. We couldn't take all those rollercoaster ups and downs.

In retrospect, I think the unsavory characters we met in the movies made us extremely grateful for our own life experiences- school and all.

It's interesting how we manage to get through life's journey by looking at those who have it worse than ourselves. My dad hit that truth home to me when he told me that someone once said, "I cried because I had no shoes, until I met a person who had no feet."

The Moore Cousins Line Up and Take A Stand

Every week we checked the Legion of Decency's Movie Ratings. If the film was deemed "Morally Unobjectionable," then we could go. If it was "Condemned," or "Morally Objectionable," we could forget about it.

One Saturday afternoon all of the Moore cousins went to see a Western at the Towne Theatre. When the Moore cousins got together, my sister Rita, being the oldest, was in charge of us all.

We were all settled down enjoying our popcorn and candy, with our feet stuck firmly to the floor. This was the life! Shortly into the movie, however, my sister whispered something to my cousin Margie and I. "Look at that saloon lady's dress. It's too low!" We hadn't noticed and I didn't think it was any worse than Miss Kitty's dresses on Gunsmoke every week. But Rita was insistent that this Wild West woman was immodest and she was going to get us all out of there! So we whispered down the lane into each little Moore ear that we were about to take a stand against such movie immorality! The news that we were "shocked and appalled" and we're all going to leave in a huff, went from Rita to Margie and down the line to Cathy, Terri, Patty, Jerry and Eddie. We were about to teach them a lesson they would never forget.

We planned to make a grand exit and march out in a united front

Shut Up and Get in Line

against this Levittown Theatre that was corrupting the morals of minors. Boy were we fired up! The long line of outraged little Moore relatives had begun their protest and the world would know that we were fed up!

As we paraded down the aisle, making comments about "how we didn't have to take this," we headed for the exit door, stormed out- and SLAMMED it hard! We fully expected the entire audience to get up and follow us out. Outside we continued our grumblings about the filth that we had just witnessed and were proud as peacocks that we were such outstanding children. We knew that there was no better group than ours. There was even talk about the possibility of being on the front page of the Bucks County Courier Times as role models for the rest of the town. "If we call right now," we reasoned, "We could be in the headlines of today's paper!" But none of us had a dime to make the call.

How proud our parents would be for our courage, high morals and quick thinking! Instead, they were mad that we left the theatre early and didn't get our money's worth.

Chapter 21

"IN THE LINE OF DUTY"
Sister vs. Paul

Along with being a product of Catholic Schools, I also became a teacher in Catholic School. The stark contrast between my school days and the Religious education I taught was extreme. By the end of the sixties, the Catechism was taken out of Catholic Schools. I think this was a sad day for Catholic education. The children growing up without the Baltimore Catechism did not have the benefit of learning the truths of the faith in such a way as to be repeated and recalled by memory each year. By memorizing these truths, so crucial to the development of an informed conscience, the faith becomes alive and actually helps the person travel along the path of right thinking for which he was created.

We learned from the Catechism as children what we were doing here on this earth. We learned that our purpose here is to know, love and serve God in this world so we can be happy with Him in Heaven. We learned all the important character traits that we would endeavor to acquire and even received report card grades for them. And yes, we even learned about Heaven and Hell. Did we ever! Once, a public school kid asked me why I was going to Catholic School. I said, "My mom wants me to learn what hell is." I still tremble at the description of hell given to us by our fifth grade nun. "It's a huge sea of fire, where

Shut Up and Get in Line

you will spend eternity. You will never leave that fire. You can't swim out, even if you are constantly screaming in pain." I wonder how many fallen away Catholics came back to the faith because of their early teaching about Hell? I heard that the devil's greatest accomplishment is convincing people that he doesn't exist. (His second biggest accomplishment was splitting the Church into over 65,000 different denominations. Can you imagine the strength of Christianity had we all remained together?)

The President of our class every year was usually Paul, the smartest kid in the class. Paul had many good qualities. He was very upstanding and a natural leader.

One Monday in fifth grade, our very strict and no nonsense teacher told everyone to stand if he had not attended Benediction on Friday evening. ("Uh-oh," I thought, "I don't like the sound of this.") With trepidation, most of us stood up. Sister went down the rows asking why we hadn't attended. The students who lived near the school could have walked and since Sister knew where everyone lived, it was the ones who lived closest who were on the chopping block. When it was my turn to give my excuse, I explained, "Stir, I didn't have a ride." She said, "Sit down." Whew! I was in the clear. Time for me to relax and watch the poor lazy things get their just due. (I knew they should have been there, but I bet they were all out playing!) Sister was not in a good mood because our class had such poor attendance at church. It was Paul's turn to give his excuse. Paul was not the typical fifth grader. He had unusual integrity and goodness. In fact, he was like a little Apostle. Now Sister knew that Paul lived right around the corner from the school, so she was not happy to see him standing. "Well Sir, you live close to the church. Why weren't you there?" I was feeling a bit uneasy. "I had family responsibilities, Sister."(Paul was boldly going where no child had ever gone before.) "What family responsibilities?" Sister questioned. Paul responded, "It's my family duty to walk the dog." There was a collective gasp from the class. I knew trouble was coming. Paul was very serious about his family duties and Sister was very serious about going to church. Sister told Paul to come up to the front of the room. Aw, this can't be good, I thought.

Sister began, "Now Mister, what is more important, going to see Jesus reposed in the Blessed Sacrament or walking your dog?" I pleaded with him in my head, "Paul, get yourself out of this!" Paul's face was turning red. I wanted him to give the correct answer. "Well Sister," explained Paul, "My duties as a son and a brother, and my family job is to walk the dog." NO PAUL NO! I screamed in my head. Sister turned bright red as she began winding up. Then she let Paul have it! Whack! Poor brave little Paul. He had such an honorable and convicted spirit, and so did Sister. The two stubborn and principled people had met their match. The rest of us poor fools sat their shaking and feeling sorry for Paul. I hope he got an A in Courage on his report card. I don't know what transpired that evening but Paul returned the next day and apologized to Sister and the class.

I have to say that after the incident with Paul, I was mad at Sister for awhile, about thirty-five years. Then I thought about all the good things that she taught us. I realized I would have to forgive her anyway. If we don't forgive others, we won't be forgiven either. I read this verse from the Bible and it knocked some sense into me; "In the same way you judge others, you will be judged and with the measure you use, it will be measured to you." Anyway, maybe Sister was having a really bad day, maybe that's the only way she thought she could make her point. Maybe

Shut Up and Get in Line

she was brought up that way herself. Corporal punishment was big when she was growing up. Then I started to feel sorry for Sister. After all, how would I feel having to wear a hot, heavy, woolen habit every day, a long veil, lace-up heels and starched sheets of cardboard digging into my forehead, neck and face?

(My mom and dad both went to school in the thirties when corporal punishment was popular. My mom tells the story of a day when she had to pick up her older brother's homework in the eighth grade classroom. She said that there was a tiny little nun standing on a stool and all the boys were standing in a line waiting their turn to be hit. None of them were talking back or being disrespectful. All knew that they deserved it and quietly took their medicine.)

I just felt grateful that we didn't have to wear those big dunce caps that were worn in the Little Rascal movies.

Parents have a great way of rationalizing any unjust punishment we may have received as children. Anytime we felt that we did not deserve the punishment we were getting, our parents would reason, "Well, if you think you didn't deserve it this time, use it toward sometime when you did deserve it and didn't get caught." Extrapolating on that idea over a lifetime, many of us may have gotten off way too easy.

Okay, the nuns and priests aren't perfect. No one is. In my child's mind, I thought they were supposed to be. I forgot that they were human beings and I put them on some kind of a pedestal for so long that wasn't meant for the rest of us. Why did I expect that the nuns and priests would be perfect when the Lord's own hand-picked original twelve Apostles weren't even perfect? I was finding out that nuns and priests do eat and sleep and they can even sin like the rest of us. But they have made an unusual, special and outstanding commitment to offer their lives to God. Sure, they will get tempted and fall sometimes, but that's human nature. They should be admired for their great faith and dedication.

When my parents heard that someone had talked back to Sister, they said, "He'll never amount to anything." The last I heard, Paul was written up in "Who's Who of American Businesses" and is a big Executive for Price- Waterhouse.

> "And all men are ready to pass judgment on the priest as if he was not a being clothed with flesh or one who inherited a human nature."
>
> Saint John Chrysostom

Chapter 22

"LINE OF DEMARCATION"
Parent-Teacher Conference

Sometimes our parents had to show up at the school for Parent-Teacher Conferences and review our report cards with our teachers. When I was in fifth grade, I was in shock when my mother got all dolled up for a conference with my strict teacher, a nun. I knew how modesty and good sense in clothing was admired by the nuns and there was nothing in my mom's attire that was fitting into that category. My mother was all decked out wearing a fancy dress with spike heels, a huge lace hat, big beaded jewelry and wrapped around her neck was the most unbelievable thing- a fur stole made out of about seven little fox heads!!! When I saw her ready to go, I screamed, "NOOOOOO!! Don't go like that!!" I was running around having conniptions and trying to convince her how embarrassed I was. I even used one of her favorite lines, "You're going to queer our good name." She said, "Get in the car, we're leaving." My dad and mom just ignored my begging. "PLLEEASSE! You don't understand!!!" There was no hope for me. (I wish they would have given me that bomb shelter I asked for at Christmas. I could have hid in there.) They made me get in the car. I was mortified. I sat on the floor of the back seat and cried the whole way groaning, "I'll get in trouble because they'll think you're a movie star or something." I could barely breathe between my sobs as all those little fox eyes were staring at me. While I carried on during that car ride, the two of them acted as if everything was right with the world in that get up and behaved as though it was normal to have animal heads wrapped all around her neck.

The only thing that quieted me down was when my mom said, "Sister better not give me a bad report about you or you'll really have something to cry about. Oh no, now what? If anyone knew what a goofball I was, it was Sister! But then again, maybe things could go well for me. Once Sister gets a load of my mother with my dad standing proudly beside her and the foxes, she might feel pity for me.

Luckily, everything turned out fine. Sister gave my parents a good report and she never even mentioned the ghastly ensemble to me.

Shut Up and Get in Line

Psalms 50 Verse 12 tells us- "If I were hungry, I would not ask you for food, for the world and everything in it is Mine." Then in Verse 13 he tells us, "Giving thanks is the sacrifice that honors me, and I will surely save all who obey Me."

God will not be outdone in generosity. He loves each of His children as if he/she were the only one. He has given us more than we could have ever imagined. We need to thank Him and praise Him every day for His generous gifts. Saint Paul of the Cross advises us to look around and notice His gifts and praise our magnificent Creator.-"Listen to the sermon preached to you by the flowers, the trees and the shrubs, the sky and the whole world. Notice how they preach to you a sermon full of love, of praise of God, and how they invite you to glorify the sublimity of that sovereign Artist who has given them being."[1]

When Our Lord says, "Ask and you shall receive, seek and you shall find, knock and it shall be opened to you," (Matthew 7:7), we must take that to heart and realize how much He wants to give us. Sometimes as a mother, I question myself as to whether I remembered to teach my children certain lessons. Did I cover all the bases? Did I tell them everything I needed to tell them? What if I don't get the chance to tell them anything else? I thought the same way about God. Had I remembered to tell Him how grateful I am for everything and to thank Him from the bottom of my heart? What if I die before I get the chance to say all that I feel?

"LET ME TELL YOU NOW"

I asked for countless blessings
And received each treasured one,
Dear Father, let me thank You-
Especially for Your Son.

I sought and found the answers
As I followed your Beacon of Light,
Ever gently guiding my footsteps,
I learned of Your power and might.

I knocked at the door of Truth
And it opened wide to me,
You breathed life onto the pages of my
Bible- so I might see.

Before my days are over
And my chance to give is done,
Let me give my heart and soul
To You, Almighty One.

The majesty of creation
Is too much for the soul to bear,
Let me praise You now on my knees
For Your splendor and infinite care.

Shut Up and Get in Line

For all the times that I hurt You
And caused You sadness and pain
Let me say now that I am sorry,
Please Father, forgive me again.

The day You call me home, Lord
Will be too late to say,
"Let me beg You now for Your mercy."
I will cry out for mercy today.

And when I knock the last time
May You open Your Heavenly door,
Then I'll tell You again that I love You
And praise You forevermore.

Chapter 23

"SMILE LINES"
Ralph Cracks Up the Class

It's funny how we are able to control ourselves in certain situations when absolutely necessary. One day Sister called Ralph up to the board. There was a big hanging map of the world and Sister was asking us questions about the map. She handed the pointer to Ralph and said, "Show us the equator, Ralph." Ralph took the pointer and responded, "Well, it starts up here in Canada and it curves all the way down here through the middle states down into the ocean." Ralph used the pointer and swirled a crooked line all the way down the map. While Ralph was giving his hysterical answer, I was silently laughing so hard at my desk that tears were rolling down my cheeks. If Sister were to look at me during this ridiculous moment, she would have seen an expressionless tear-stained face. I'm sure there were forty other poker faced students trying to stifle their own infectious laughter, all terrified to crack a smile. Ordinarily, anyone not capable of controlling his laughter would find himself in front of the class being scolded for making fun of the less fortunate. But this time it was different. Ralph was so funny that Sister herself lost her composure and actually laughed out loud! Before you knew it, the entire class, including Ralph was laughing along with Sister. What a relief! That was one of the few times that I had looked at a nun as an actual real live human being. It was

Shut Up and Get in Line

surprising to me that they had emotions just like the rest of us.

(Of course some screwball had to ruin the tender moment that Sister was sharing with the class. There's always one that has to go overboard. When we were all enjoying ourselves in the midst of all the hilarity, one of the boys acted as if he was laughing so hard that he threw himself out of his desk and fell onto the floor. He got all of us in trouble for his lack of self-control. I was hoping that he would be expelled. Just when Sister was warming up to us, he ruined everything!)

Watching Sister laugh was reminiscent of a time when two of the nuns were outside working on a Saturday. We were playing kickball on the field near the convent. The ball rolled near the nuns and one of them kicked it!!!! We were so stunned! Everyone ran around jumping up and down screaming and telling everyone that "Sister kicked the ball! Sister kicked the ball!" We just couldn't believe it. We thought they didn't have it in them to have fun or they just weren't allowed to participate in such triviality as sports. The sight of that laughing nun kicking the ball in her apron was a happy sight to behold. Later on, when we told the kids who weren't there about it, they didn't believe us.

> "Joy, with peace, is the sister of charity. Serve the Lord with laughter."[1]
>
> Padre Pio

Babs Takes A Spin

One lazy summer afternoon, my friend Babs and I were looking for something to do. I was in seventh grade and Babs was in sixth. We decided to take a stack of her "Archie" comic books and read them outside. Babs made each of us a glass of cherry Kool-Aid and she managed to scrounge up two pieces of Bazooka bubble gum. Armed with our goodies, we headed out to sit on the curb. Babs had a better idea. "Hey, let's sit in the car with our stuff!" I jumped in and dug through the pile to see which of Archie's adventures I wanted to read again. Babs wasn't content. "Hey, do ya wanna listen to the radio?" "I guess, but you can't turn it on." I reminded her. "Wait here. I'll be right back," she said. Babs returned in a few moments jiggling the car keys. "Check it out!" Babs bravely exclaimed. "Are you allowed to turn on the radio?" I asked. "Don't sweat it. They're takin a nap and Mary Ann ain't home." She responded. So we listened to our favorite stations, WIBG and WFIL for awhile until Babs became bored again. She began to look all around as if trying to get her bearings. "I wonder what it would feel like to move the car down the driveway?" She seemed to be thinking out loud. "No way!" I warned. "I'm just gonna back it up," she said. "I'm getting out!" I threatened. "Wait!" Babs tried to bargain with me. "I have a surprise for you, if you don't chicken out." She had my attention now. I loved surprises. "I'm getting you something," she promised, "And it has to do with ice-cream." "That's really big of you, Babs. You get us ice-cream all the time." (Both of Babs' parents worked and she was in the habit of dipping into her dad's coin collection whenever the ice-cream man came around. She was a very generous girl and she loved treating all the neighborhood kids.) "This is different,"

Shut Up and Get in Line

explained Babs. My mom is taking us to Greenwood Dairies and you're getting a Pig's Dinner!" "What?! Really?!"

This was outrageous! A Pig's Dinner was an ice-cream lover's dream come true! Ten scoops of ice-cream in any flavors you chose, every topping ever invented, gobs of whipped cream and served in a big trough! Whoever was capable of eating a whole one was awarded with a badge that said, "I Was a Pig at Greenwood Dairies." This was an honor we had all aspired to, but I never dreamed I would be getting the opportunity already!

Babs looked around again and bragged, "I can do this. It's only a few feet." With those words, she turned on the car and I dove for the floor in an uncontrollable siege of laughter. She backed the car down the driveway! I was all set to get off the floor, but Babs was so proud of her newfound driving ability, that she pointed the car toward the street and decided to take a spin around the block! Held hostage by fear, exhilaration, and laughter, my side-splitting gut was about to explode. "Let me out! Let me out!" I protested, knowing that she wasn't about to stop. This was the best day ever! I was hiding on the floor and there I stayed, fearful that someone would see me and my eleven year-old driver.

Seatbelts weren't an issue back then. Her car didn't have them. Not that I could have used them anyway, all curled up on the floor.

After maneuvering around several parked cars, we finally returned to the safety of the driveway. What a relief when she finally turned that car off and took out the key!

Trying to regain my composure was no easy task. Once I would calm myself and finally stop laughing, I thought about our neighborhood jaunt again and I would lose it once more. This went on and on. Then I remembered what made it all worthwhile, my own big Pig's Dinner! "So, when is your mom taking us to Greenwood Dairies?" I asked eagerly. Babs replied, "She'll never take us there. She'll say it costs too much." "What?!" In my mind I could see my Pig's Dinner melting away. I was livid and so I threatened, "You better get her to take us there, if you don't want her to find out about all this! She's gonna kill you!!" "Not if she thinks you did the driving," Babs shot back. What?? Oh swell, I just risked my life on a wild joy ride with this imbecile and now she's threatening to twist the whole thing around and make me the villain! Before I could continue voicing my outrage, Babs reached for an Archie comic book on the top of the pile. "Look at that Jughead," she laughed, "What a jackass." The two of us broke out in another round of uproarious laughter. Friends again, all was forgotten. Two giddy little school girls were in the grips of their next big laugh.

Chapter 24

"EVERY CLOUD HAS A SILVER LINING"
May Procession

What makes May so beautiful is that it is the month of Mary. It is when we honor her for being our devoted and loving Mother. What would May have been without remembering our dear, sweet Mother, our greatest advocate who intercedes for us with her Divine Son? Every day in May we could bring flowers of all kinds for our Lady, flowers of the fairest and flowers of the rarest. Lovely fragrant flowers surrounded our classroom statue of Mary and our full hearts really were swelling with love for her. Through the years, our Sisters and Teachers spoke with such love about Mary that their strong feelings were contagious and we all learned in no uncertain terms how blessed we all were to have such a special and Holy Mother.

Our annual school May Procession was a joyful and touching event where all of the children from every grade came together to crown the Blessed Mother, bring her flowers and sing beautiful songs to her. All of the First Communion children wore white dresses and veils and the boys wore blue suits. The Confirmation Class came dressed in their Sunday best. The remaining children wore their school uniforms.

When I was in eighth grade, the May Procession was held outside. This was usually the case if the weather was nice. It was a beautiful Spring day and the entire school was facing the church. The statue of Our Lady and the May Queen and her Court along with the Priest, all stood in front. The Church had stained glass window panes. There was someone in the church who opened a window and pointed a big camera through it. The children were distracted and kept looking at the person who was moving from window to window taking pictures. My class was laughing as we watched the big camera that was making all the noise and interrupting the solemn Procession. It was the Principal who went into the church to correct the culprit. I was humiliated when the Principal came walking out of the church escorting my father and his new toy, the huge Kodak Super eight instamatic movie camera. Nooooo! Not him! I screamed in my head. How could he do this to me? I wanted to melt into the macadam. I think I got my just reward because I was all set to start laughing at the sorry soul who was being scolded.

My third grade brother was equally embarrassed. Of course all of the eyes of my fellow classmates were on me. Some laughed and some had a look of pity on their faces, obviously very relieved that it wasn't their dad who was in trouble with the Principal.

Whenever I see pictures of that day, I remember what an emotional time it was for me. Thankfully, I had someone there comforting me. Our beautiful Blessed Mother, Queen of Heaven and Earth, has been holding my hand since I was a youngster, and has thankfully, never let it go.

Imagine what kind of world it would be if all the girls and women used the Blessed Virgin Mary as their role model. Goodness, Purity, Gentleness, Kindness and Strength of Character would shine in all of our girls. They would not be copying negative behaviors, immorality or impropriety from any of the rock stars, movie stars or TV personalities in our culture today. They would only imitate the virtuous, positive example and lovely traits of their perfect Heavenly Mother, the only woman who deserves to be called, and lives up to the beautiful name, Madonna.

> "Mother Dear, lend me your heart. I look for it each day to pour my troubles into."
> Saint Gemma Galgani

These lovely sentiments were written by Paul Cross (pen name- Justin Mulcahy, CF.) He uses beautiful imagery and expresses the close and special relationship between Our Lord and Our Lady.

AD JESUM PER MARIAM

Mary the Dawn, Christ the Perfect Day;
Mary the Gate, Christ the Heavenly Way!
Mary the Root, Christ the Mystic Vine;
Mary the Grape, Christ the Sacred Wine!
Mary the Wheat, Christ the Living Bread;
Mary the Stem, Christ the Rose Blood-red!
Mary the Font, Christ the Cleansing Flood;
Mary the Cup, Christ the Saving Blood!
Mary the Temple, Christ the Temple's Lord;
Mary the Shrine, Christ the God adored!
Mary the Beacon, Christ the Haven's Rest;
Mary the Mirror, Christ the Vision Blest!
Mary the Mother, Christ the Mother's Son;
By all things blest while endless ages run. Amen
(This piece is actually considered one of the top ten Catholic Hymns.)

Chapter 25

"SETTING BOUNDARY LINES"
Stay With the Program

Some classes as a whole need stricter discipline than others. Older children still need teachers who are good disciplinarians to help them learn self-control. Without discipline, chaos reigns. Sometimes we witness this when a substitute teacher takes over a class. Children know instinctively when and who to take advantage of, and they usually do. Because I became a teacher myself, I learned this lesson first hand.

One of my first jobs as a twenty-two year old teacher was to substitute for a seventh grade Biology class in a Philadelphia public school. Before the morning bell even rang, a few students opened all the animal cages! There were birds flying, hamsters running and bunnies hopping all over that lab before I was even finished reading the day's lesson plan. I quickly enlisted the help of a few serious looking students to round up the run-away zoo. The class thoroughly enjoyed themselves laughing hysterically until the Principal stopped by.

I remember being told my first year of teaching, "Don't smile until Christmas." When I began teaching in an inner city public school, I was warned, "These children mistake kindness for weakness."

Teaching Sisters and Priests have developed their own styles and they do what works best for them. I remember two extremely mild mannered and soft spoken nuns I had in grade school. One was so beautiful and quiet that I think she had trouble controlling our primary grade class. The other Sister, who also had a beautiful countenance, taught us the first part of seventh grade. Because of her gentle nature and quiet manner, our class took advantage of her and she had to be replaced. The nun who replaced her took no nonsense from us and we shaped up in a hurry.

Due to the rigorous training, matter of fact approach to life and uncompromising manner which our Sisters and Priests implemented, those of us who were taught by them are all the better for it.

Just as in the secular world, there are countless personality types, so too there are in the convents and rectories of this world. Perhaps God gives us glimpses of Himself in the personality traits of His creatures. To one He gives a gentle spirit, to another, a voice that speaks with firmness and authority. Still others He bestows with the gifts of humor, compassion or patience. Perhaps some years we needed the sweet spirit of a tenderhearted Sister. Other years, with our growing rebelliousness, we clearly needed a firmer hand to guide and tame us. Thank God for the good nuns, the sweet ones and the strict, no-nonsense ones. The strong Sisters and Priests who gave us precise and definite rules to follow from which there would be no deviating, are just who we needed when we needed them. We learned from each Sister, Teacher and Priest that had authority over us. Perhaps we learned joy from one and orderliness from another, kindness from one and self-control from another. Many times we have witnessed such profound Faith in our priests, nuns and teachers that they became the impetus for our own spiritual growth.

In many ways we benefited from the unique qualities that each one possessed.

Hand-picked by God for the care and keeping of His souls on earth, they are a special breed in the love story between God and man. By responding to God's call, they are transforming the world one soul at a time.

I often wondered as a child, why would a person choose this kind of life? How could they give up their whole life and all of their good times? What did the nuns and priests know that we didn't know? The priests and the nuns get it. They are on fire with the love of God and have an interior understanding of the truths of the Faith. They have received a great gift from God in their vocation. Because they have listened to the inner stirrings of their hearts and obeyed God's instructions, we are all blessed.

> "There are so many souls that would attain sanctity if only they were well directed."[1]
>
> Saint Therese of Lisieux

Chapter 26

"TOP OF THE LINE FASHION FOR THE IN-CROWD"
Wearing White and Looking Good

One thing I noticed in the family albums is that for all the important events, white was being worn, symbolizing purity of heart. The babies at their Baptisms wore white. First Holy Communion dresses are white. Confirmation gowns and wedding gowns for the Sacrament of Matrimony are white. Priests wear white to receive Holy Orders. I imagine us all at the end of the world in a big long line walking into Heaven in our white robes. We learn from Revelations 7,12 that in Heaven white robes will be worn… "After this I looked, and there was an enormous crowd- no one could count all the people! They were from every race, tribe, nation and language; and they stood in front of the throne and of the Lamb, dressed in white robes and holding palm branches in their hands. They called out in a loud voice! "Salvation comes from our God who sits on the throne, and from the Lamb! All the Angels stood around the throne, the elders and the four living creatures. Then they threw themselves face downward in front of the throne and worshiped God, saying, "Amen! Praise, glory, wisdom, thanksgiving, honor, power and might belong to our God forever and ever! Amen!"

I think of a big, long Communion Line, just like the ones we stood in so many times on earth, with people of all races, sizes and shapes. (Only this line goes on as far as the eye can see) Each one so loved and cherished by their Creator. I see people I knew and loved; my relatives, friends and classmates and some I had never seen before. But we were all brothers and sisters and I could feel our strong bond. I recognize Noah and his family and all the Saints I learned about in school. I see the Apostles and Moses. I recognize Pope John Paul ll, Elijah, David and Joseph. There are so many relatives I see from Adam's line, I could never count the number. They are all in complete conformity, peaceful beyond all understanding and in perfect ecstasy.

Revelations 7:13-14- "And one of the elders answered saying unto me, What are these which are arrayed in white robes? And whence came they? And I said to him, Sir, thou knowst. And he said to me, these are they which came out of great tribulation and have washed their robes and made them white in the blood of the Lamb."

Wow! Could it be any clearer to us? Just think- We could be next in line to stand before the Judgment Seat! When your eternity is on the line like that, what goes through your head? Consider what is at stake. Were our parents, nuns and priests strict enough with us? Did we learn to be strict with ourselves and live in conformity to God's will? Thank God we were raised in the faith and learned the true meaning of life and our purpose in it.

The Sacraments, which were instituted by Christ to give grace, help us focus on Him. Each time a Sacrament is received, we are remembering, honoring, praising, loving and glorifying Him. The reception of the Sacraments is a wonderful preparation and fertile training ground for our Heavenly home. In light of Scripture, we see a striking resemblance in our Sacramental life here on earth and our eternal life in Heaven- Even down to our clothing.

Since the Lord created us for Himself, our souls long for Him. His gentle presence tugs at our heartstrings always drawing us closer to Him. As the Body of Christ, we have been given every necessity and all the directions through Mother Church to lead us sure-footed along the path that leads to our Heavenly home. Jesus said, "I will not leave you orphans." He has provided a Church to lead us in and has comforted us in such a way as to leave us His own precious Body and Blood as food for our journey.

> "Without the Holy Eucharist there would be no happiness in this world, and life wouldn't be bearable."[1]
> Saint John Vianney

Chapter 27

"FORBIDDEN LINE"
Permanent Record in Jeopardy

In eighth grade, I had to stay home from school for a week because I was sick. The doctor said he wanted to test me for Mononucleosis. "What's mononucleosis, Mom?" (I could hardly pronounce it.) My mother's answer made me want to crawl away and hide under the nearest rock. "The doctor said it's the Kissing Disease." What in the world was she saying? "What do you mean, Mom?" I was horrified. She repeated, "It's the Kissing Disease." My mind was racing trying to process this bizarre new information and the implied accusation. I never even said hi to a boy. Everyone knew that after seventh grade, the boys and girls were separated and we never had any contact with them at all. Our classrooms were separate and our playgrounds were separate. We weren't to talk to them and they weren't to talk to us. The nearest I had ever gotten to a boy is when they came around to sell orange drinks and soft pretzels in the afternoon, or during Mass when the Altar boy helped Father at Communion. (Even if I did have a nickel for a pretzel, I would never have bought one from a boy! He would think I was a big pig.)

"Mom, there must be some mistake. He's wrong." She shot back, "Are you calling the doctor a liar?" "No, but I didn't kiss anyone!" I

Shut Up and Get in Line

defended myself. "Well," Mom said, "He did say that you can also get it from dirty spoons or sharing utensils." Hooray!! I thought. I'm not a loose girl, just a slob. I was off the hook. I would not have been able to bear it if my parents thought I had kissed a boy. As it turned out, it wasn't Mono after all, just a virus. The doctor called one afternoon with the good news and said that I should go outside to get some fresh air. My mother was so happy, actually gleeful. "Great News!" she sang. "You don't have Mono! So, go outside and have a ball!" Have a ball?? What's with mom? I was thrilled too though, and I'll never forget those words, "Have a ball!" Neato! I ran out, overjoyed to be outside again. I got on my bike and headed right up to the school to watch my team's softball game.

The next morning in school, my very strict teacher said firmly, "Catherine Moore!" "Yes, Sister," I responded. "See me after prayers!" Sister said. Aw-Shhucks! This doesn't sound good, I thought. I wasn't in school for a whole week. Well, wasn't this a fine how do you do? My mind began to wander during prayers- Why does Sister want to see me? What did I do? Did I drift off course in Voyages in English? It was probably one of those darn compound- complex sentences that I didn't diagram right. Maybe it was a history test that I screwed up. What did I care about the discoveries of Cortez or Balboa? I was thirteen now, making new discoveries of my own and developing my own interests. I had to concentrate on important current events like the news and excitement of my big sister Rita going on television to dance on American Bandstand. This show wasn't made in some remote corner of the earth like California, but right in Philadelphia, our own back yard. Around that time I was also making plans for my own trip of a lifetime. I would soon be headed to a place that I waited eight years to see. Our whole class would be traveling to Willow Grove Amusement Park for our eighth grade trip! I could hardly wait to climb on board The Thunderbolt, that big roller-coaster in the sky that I heard about so much. Goodbye to the Whip, that bogus ride that came around our neighborhood on the back of a truck, with little cars running around an oval track. That truck driver would be getting no more quarters from me. I was on my way to greener pastures.

In fact, pretty soon I would be leaving all this baby stuff behind and riding into a whole new spectacular world where all the cool people were. I was going to High School!

Could it be that I forgot to underline one of my headings of Name, Date and Subject in red? No way! I would have certainly caught something that outlandish.

Word problems- that must be it! I bet I messed up on my answers last week. Well, all the Saints were being invoked and prayers were almost over. Taking that long walk up to Sister's desk was torture, not even suspecting what was wrong. "Yes, Stir?" I asked. Sister turned to me. "You were absent yesterday." "Yes, Stir." "Why?" Sister questioned. I answered, "Stir, I had to take a test because the doctor thought I may have mononucleosis. He called in the afternoon and said that I didn't have it, and told my mom that I should go out and get some fresh air. So, I went to the field to watch my softball game." I jumped back when Sister shouted, "TRUANT, YOU WERE TRUANT! YOU ARE FORBIDDEN TO LEAVE THE HOUSE WHEN YOU ARE ABSENT FROM SCHOOL! Our Principal may have to report you to the Authorities." Oh NO, I thought, what will become of me, and more importantly, my permanent record!?

All day long, I pictured myself sitting in jail with my whole family.

Shut Up and Get in Line

It's no wonder, too. When I got home that afternoon and told my mother what Sister said, her response was, "TRUANT? Oh my God, you were TRUANT? The Police are going to get us? Why the hell did you go to that school?" I cried, "Because you said I could go out and I wanted to watch the game." "Well you little rippobate of hell! What did you bring on us?" she yelled. (I never knew what a rippobate was, but it can't be good. I'm thinking that she meant "reprobate" but it always came out "rippobate.")

My mom was about to utter her favorite line and I knew it was coming, "What will the neighbors think?" she wailed. It seemed we were always staging our lives around the neighbors and how they would view us. We wanted to be the best family on the whole street. My dad's standard reply was always, "They're worse than us." I never found out how they were worse than us, but it always made me feel better.

We never did do any jail time due to my truancy. Mom had the doctor write a note explaining everything to Sister, so we were once again respected citizens of the community and "the pillars of the church."

Chapter 28

"ON THE FRONT LINES"
The Funniest Kid in the Class

There was a boy in my class at St. Joseph the Worker School who was the funniest, yet the nicest kid in the class. He never made fun of anyone but himself. He would say the most hysterical and witty things in a self-deprecating way. His name was John and he lived with his family on the school grounds in the old rectory. His dad was the same as John, wonderful and kind to everyone. His dad was a brilliant engineer, but also fixed things at our school and worked around the property. I loved to see him walking around outside. He was always so peaceful. Later, when we became teenagers, a bunch of us would hang out in John's basement and we were always welcomed by his parents. John was an Altar Boy, and because he lived so close to the church, he was the one who was always called to serve Mass in the bad weather. I believe this opportunity would serve him well later in life. This wonderful, kind and funny little boy grew up to be a beautiful and holy Franciscan Friar of the Renewal, Father Conrad Osterhout, CFR. (I never knew that someone who was so funny was allowed to become a Priest!) To this day, Father Conrad carries the joy and love of the Lord to all. Father Conrad has great courage and compassion for the poor and unborn. He inspired many to join the group, "Helpers of God's

Shut Up and Get in Line

Precious Infants." Once a month this group attends Mass, Adoration and Benediction. Then they walk to the nearby abortion clinic to pray the Rosary. What a powerful sensation. You can actually feel the battle between good and evil at these prayer vigils. Father has educated thousands of people with the facts about abortion. When I first heard the statistics and the actual numbers, it was a stunning and enlightening revelation. The shocking truth is that there were over fifty-million people killed in abortions, more than all those killed in all the wars throughout our history. This is mind boggling. Our society is filled with non-thinkers. The deliberate murder of our innocent fellow human beings is a cruel and egregious abomination and a sad and sorrowful statement about our culture. A culture that devalues life is desensitized to the point where no one is safe. We must learn from those wiser than ourselves. The brilliance of Pope John Paul ll shines forth in this enlightened thought, "As believers, how can we fail to see that abortion is a terrible rejection of God's gift of life and love?" If God Himself would not do such a thing, how can we? Isaiah 66:9 reminds us- "Shall I bring a mother to the point of birth and yet not let her child be born? Says the Lord; or shall I who allows her to conceive, yet close her womb? Says your God." Who are we to tamper with God's creation?

I saw the most beautiful video on EWTN of a song called, "This is My Body." It was so moving and clearly teaches us that our bodies belong to the Lord, and we are to use them and all His creation for his honor and glory. If this video were shown to all high school students, I believe it would change hearts.

Father Conrad stands up for the innocent unborn. He was their voice and their hero when most of us were ignoring their lonely and sorrowful plight. Because of Father's courageous stance, he spent two years in prison for defending precious life. Along with six other Voices for the Unborn, Father and the group became known as The Allentown Seven and were taken to court for praying outside of an abortion clinic.

Father Conrad became a prisoner for defending human life. He then carried Christ's love to the troubled men who lived within those prison walls and became a blessing to them.

In his insightful and bestselling book, "The Cross at Ground Zero", Father Benedict Groeschel, CFR writes: "Do you know that abortion is the most protected right in the United States? I deny absolutely that there is equal justice before law. A physician cannot give an aspirin to a minor without parental consent, but he can perform an abortion on a minor without consent of the parents.

"I have my own personal grievance against the federal and state governments, which ignored saboteurs and terrorists who had been operating for several years in the United States and who attempted to destroy the World Trade Center in 1993. Do you know who the government was watching? They were watching me and many others who are opposed to abortion. Some of us went to jail."

"I was arrested, along with the very saintly Bishop George Lynch, eighty-three years old, and (at that time) Brother Fidelis Moscinski, who is now a priest in our Franciscan community. All we did was say the rosary. We didn't block anything. As we prayed at the entrance to the driveway of the abortion center, we stood on the public sidewalk. You could have driven a motorcycle between us. But we did deliberately stop walking during our prayer vigil. We knelt down to say the rosary on the sidewalk at the parking entrance."[1]

Quoting from the Holy Father's address to Ambassador Nicholson, the U.S. Ambassador to the Holy See, Father Groeschel writes: "In order to survive and prosper, democracy and its accompanying economic and political structures must be directed by a vision whose core is the God-given dignity and inalienable rights of every human being, from the moment of conception until natural death. When some lives, including those of the unborn, are subjected to the personal choices of others, no other value or right will long be guaranteed, and society will inevitably be governed by special interests and convenience.

Freedom cannot be sustained in a cultural climate that measures human dignity in strictly utilitarian terms. Never has it been more urgent to reinvigorate the moral vision and resolve essential to maintaining a just and free society.

Jesus says, "It must needs be that scandal come, but woe to that man by whom scandal shall come." (see Matthew 18:7) Abraham Lincoln cites those words in his second inaugural address, given during the depth of the Civil War. Alluding to the responsibility of the country for the injustice of slavery, he says, "Fondly, do we hope, fervently do we pray, that this mighty scourge of war may speedily pass away. Yet if God wills that it continue until all the wealth piled by the bondsman's two hundred and fifty years of unrequited toil shall be sunk, and until every drop of blood drawn with the lash shall be paid by another drawn with the sword, as was said three thousand years ago, so still it must be said 'the judgments of the Lord are true and righteous altogether." I hope Lincoln was wrong in his estimate of divine justice, because the United States of America is legally responsible for the death of fifty million defenseless, innocent children.

What has to happen before we begin to face that responsibility? Unfortunately, a great many civil and political leaders are severely morally compromised by their support of abortion and its widespread practice. And, unfortunately, religious leaders have become compromised with them. When a prophetic voice here or there tries to say something about the evils of our time- pornography, abortion, euthanasia, the corruption of the young- do we respond? Would we even listen to the prophetic voice of Jesus if He returned?"[2]

Here, Father Groeschel writes about the kind-hearted and funny little boy who grew up to become a hero for the preborn:

"One of the friars of our community, Father Conrad Osterhout, who is our novice master, is a strong pro-life advocate. He was arrested in Lehigh County, Pennsylvania, in July 1991 and imprisoned from May 1992 to May 1993 in the county jail for protesting against abortion. Father Conrad and the other protesters were charged with trespassing and given sentences from three to twelve months by a judge who said he was actually opposed to abortion personally, whatever that means. They would be released after three months if they would sign a paper and promise that they would not protest again. The treatment of Father Conrad during the time of his imprisonment is scandalous. On the feast of Corpus Christi, Father Conrad was asked to celebrate Mass with Father Harold Dagle, a priest who had been sent by the diocese of Allentown. Father Dagle asked Father Conrad to preside. Prison approval was received for both priests to offer Mass for the inmates. The officer in charge of the shift, who was called the shift commander, attended this Mass. He watched Father Conrad offer the Mass. After the other priests who had come for the Mass left, Father Conrad was taken to the prison office and charged with three criminal acts; holding an unauthorized gathering, receiving contraband (one of the priests had given him a rosary), and wearing a disguise (Mass vestments), which is considered an attempted escape. It is important to know that the guards were all there when he prepared for Mass and said Mass and that they had approved everything. Father Conrad and the others were subject to unusual restrictions during their confinement. Preparations were being made for them to work on a road gang repairing roads. They took this opportunity to protest the treatment they were receiving in the prison, which was excessively severe. As a result of this, they were put into administrative segregation and given the false reason that it was for their protection. Actually the prisoners were quite respectful to them. Father Conrad spent eleven months in this administrative segregation, which meant remaining in the cell for twenty-two hours a day. For fifteen days he was in disciplinary segregation, which meant that he had no rights at all and could not receive phone calls or have visitors.

This was not Russia during Communist times. This was not China. This was Lehigh County, Pennsylvania, which is a reasonably civilized part of the country with a large Catholic population. The pathetic part is that there was no loud protest about this kind of treatment.

"Shame, shame, shame on our country and its criminal justice system, which persecutes protesters for life and completely failed to protect our national security. Recall, if you will, that about the same time Father Conrad was in prison, the first attack on the World Trade Center occurred. If those who were in charge of our national security had pursued those attackers with the same vigilance and zeal they displayed when searching out those who protested the killing of children, it's quite possible that the World Trade Center might still be standing. These are painful facts to read, but they are facts."[3]

I remember writing to Father Conrad in prison and telling him how much I admired his courage. I told him how proud I was of him because he was such a faithful and dedicated Priest. I complimented him for being the only one in our gang that ever made anything out of themselves. He said that when he read my letter, he had a good laugh. He said, "Here I am sitting in prison and you're saying that I'm a success." Anyone who has ever met Father Conrad knows that I'm right. He has such a humble and peaceful countenance and truly does bring the love and joy of the Lord to the rest of us. He has inspired my friends and I to work in the pro-life movement and he has been a blessing to me ever since first grade. I always knew what a nice and funny kid John was, but I never knew that lovable little boy would grow up to be one of the most brilliant and successful persons I would ever meet.

> "Saying there are too many children is just like saying there are too many flowers."[4]
>
> Mother Theresa

Shut Up and Get in Line

"Will You Sing Me A Lullaby Before I Go?"

Will you sing me a lullaby before I go?
Dear Mom and Dad, I want you to know
My young heart is beating, my eyes fill with tears,
I pray that your love will conquer your fears.

God knit me here, you are my lifeline,
Will you sing to me, sweet Mother of mine?
If you do not want me, please give me away,
There are loving arms waiting that want me to stay.

You will think of me each day of your life,
And the doctor who tore me from you with his knife.
Why would you want us to suffer this pain?
If I'm lost forever, what would you gain?

My Daddy, Listen! Can you hear my screams?
Help Me! I cry for you in my dreams.
A farewell lullaby, please sing to me, Dad,
The pain is so great and I am so sad.

My heart aches to see, to feel and to touch
The Mom and Dad whom I love so much.
Will I never run, or sing or play
Or hear the kind words that mothers say?

I would love to see Grandmom and play with toys,
And hug my Daddy like most girls and boys.
To money and things my parents are drawn,
But when their arms long to hold me, I will be gone.

The tears of the Angels flood Heaven today
As I join fifty-million souls who perished this way.
We are crying our hearts out and trembling with fears,
But our screams for mercy fall on deaf ears.

Does anyone out there have compassion for me?
When you were sown in her womb, your mom let YOU be.
I am being tortured in this home that I know,
Will you sing me a lullaby before I go?

A stranger prays and sings on the street
For all the children they never will meet.
Someday in Heaven, I'll find you to say;
"Thank you for praying and singing that day.

As I lay there dying, I saw you weep,
With a sweet lullaby you sang me to sleep."
The Angels will carry me home when I cry
With millions of infants who pray in the sky

Shut Up and Get in Line

For the souls of the parents they yearned to kiss
And never will know the babies they'll miss.
My Savior awaits my arrival today,
"Vengeance is Mine," I heard the Lord say.

Your soul, Mom and Dad, you have defiled.
Oh, beg for God's mercy for killing your child!
The Angels sing lullabies at Heaven's door
And play with the Babies, our tears shed no more.

Chapter 29

"FALLING HOOK, LINE AND SINKER"
Influence of Peer Pressure

During the summer after eighth grade, John (Father Conrad) and Bob cleaned the hall after Bingo. There were huge barrels there that were used to store the Bingo equipment. Clair and Babs and I would get into the barrels and John and Bob would roll us all around. We girls were so dizzy to the point of getting nauseous, but we had to act like we were really neat in front of the boys. (That torturous teenage angst was already setting in.) It was the same sensation I had when we all went to the Wildwood Seashore with the CYO in high school. We went on a ride called the Hell Hole. It was a big round room that spun around and pinned you to the wall by centrifugal force. We were all frozen to that wall in strange positions. When I got out of that Hellhole, I was reeling with sickening lightheadedness. I knew my whole teenage world would spin out of control if I wasn't able to stop myself from publicly throwing up. As ill as I was, the power of peer pressure was even stronger. I felt the need to act cool and composed as if that would make me seem more mature. I often went to extremes to be the craziest one. I knew everyone would love the one who would do anything. When I heard all the kids excitedly declaring how great the ride had been, the lunatic that I was chimed in, "Let's go on again!"

Chapter 30

"PRECIOUS BLOODLINE"
Nurturing Our Family Tree

The parable of the Vine and the Branches is a profound and brilliant symbol of the loving family relationship between God and His people. Because the Vine is rooted in Heaven, He reaches out and extends His love free for the taking to all who abide and bear the fruit of His goodness.

It's a mind boggling experience to visit libraries, museums, great concert halls or any cultural or artistic building. When we contemplate the fact that God has given us so much- great Music, Art, Math, History and Science, we realize that His perfect Nature is truly amazing. He knows everything that was ever written in all the books in the world and He knows every melody in every piece of music that was ever composed. He is aware of what colors and textures were used in each piece of art that was ever created. He knows every math and science formula, theorem and argument that was ever stated. He can read every person's mind and innermost thoughts. He has given us every color, shade and hue and He knows how many hairs there are on each of our heads! He knows how many different types of flowers and trees He made and how many kinds of animals He created. Yet, how many times do we stop to thank Him when we enter a library or museum or building of higher learning? When we swim in His waters or climb His mountains, do we first say, "Thank You, Lord , for making this possible and creating these miraculous wonders for me to use?

These words from Job help us to realize how much we do not understand about the infinite wonders of God:

THE LORD ANSWERS JOB

Then out of the storm the Lord spoke to Job.

The Lord: "Were you there when I made the world? If you know so much, tell me about it. Who decided how large it would be? Who stretched the measuring line over it? Do you know all the answers? What holds up the pillars that support the earth? Who laid the cornerstone of the world? In the dawn of that day the stars sang together, and the heavenly beings shouted for joy.

Who closed the gates to hold back the sea when it burst from the womb of the earth? It was I who covered the sea with clouds and wrapped it in darkness. I marked the boundary for the sea and kept it behind bolted gates. I told it, "So far and no farther! Here your powerful waves must stop." Job, have you ever in all your life commanded a day to dawn? Have you ordered the dawn to seize the earth and shake the wicked from their hiding places? Daylight makes the hills and valleys stand out like the folds of a garment, clear as the imprint of a seal on clay. The light of day is too bright for the wicked and restrains them from doing violence.

Have you been to the springs in the depths of the sea? Have you walked on the floor of the ocean? Has anyone ever shown you the gates that guard the dark world of the dead? Have you any idea how big the world is? Answer me if you know.

Do you know where the light comes from or what the source of darkness is? Can you show them how far to go, or send them back again? I am sure you can, because you're so old and were there when the world was made!

Have you ever visited the storerooms, where I keep the snow and the hail? I keep them ready for times of trouble, for days of battle and war. Have you been to the place where the sun comes up, or the place from which the east wind blows?

Who dug a channel for the pouring rain and cleared the way for the thunderstorm? Who makes rain fall where no one lives? Who waters the dry and thirsty land, so that grass springs up? Does either the rain or the dew have a father? Who is the mother of the ice and the frost, which turns the waters to stone and freeze the face of the sea? Can you tie the Pleiades together or loosen the bonds that hold Orion? Can you guide the stars season by season and direct the Big and the Little Dipper? Do you know the laws that govern the skies, and can you make them apply to the earth?

Can you shout orders to the clouds and make them drench you with rain? And if you command the lightning to flash, will it come to you and say, "At your service?" Who tells the ibis when the Nile will flood, or who tells the rooster that rain will fall? Who is wise enough to count the clouds and tilt them over to pour out the rain, rain that hardens the dust into lumps?

Do you find food for lions to eat, and satisfy hungry young lions when they hide in their caves, or lie in wait in their dens? Who is it that feeds the ravens when they wander about hungry, when their young cry to me for food? Do you know when mountain goats are born? Have you watched wild deer give birth? Do you know how long they carry their young? Do you know the time for their birth? Do you know when they will crouch down and bring their young into the world? In the wilds their young grow strong; they go away and don't come back."

Job 38-40-1, 2

There is no end to the awesome works of our wondrous Creator.

God uses a variety of different means to draw His creatures closer to Himself. Some of us are touched by lovely music. When I hear the beautiful hymn that I learned as a child, "O Sacred Heart," I am completely blown away. My mother is touched when she looks at the picture of the "Divine Mercy." She feels as though she is transported to a different plane. Others are transformed when they contemplate God's beautiful creation, the flowers, mountains, stars or ocean. Sometimes Our Lord uses people or something we read that will cause us to seek Him more deeply. We need to be open, listening and watching, so we know how He is calling us to Himself. Let us never neglect to thank and praise Him every day for all of His glorious gifts.

In this beautiful poem by Joseph Mary Plunkett, we can see and feel how completely enmeshed our Lord is throughout all creation.

Shut Up and Get in Line

"I SEE HIS BLOOD UPON THE ROSE"

I see His blood upon the rose
And in the stars the glory of His eyes,
His body gleams amid eternal snow,
His tears fall from the skies.

I see His face in every flower,
The thunder and the singing of the birds
Are but His voice- and carven by His power
Rocks are His written words.

All pathways by His feet are worn
His strong heart stirs the ever-beating sea,
His crown of thorns is twined with every thorn,
His cross is every tree.

Chapter 31

"OUR LIFELINE"
The Holy Eucharist

"In one day the Eucharist will make you produce more for the glory of God than a whole lifetime without it."[1]

                                      Saint Peter Julian Eynard

The loving miracle of the Holy Eucharist is the most perfect and brilliant gift of our Divine Lord and Redeemer. To be able to consume His very Body and Blood, as our lifeline, almost transcends our human understanding. What a comforting and beautiful, Heavenly consolation to know we are brothers and sisters with the precious Body and Blood of Jesus surging through our veins. The reception of such a sublime gift requires complete reverence which is reflected in our gestures and dress. We get a good sense of the empyreal right here and now every time we receive the Sacrament of the Holy Eucharist, since it truly is Paradise on earth.

Saint Thomas Aquinas writes lovingly about the gift of the Holy Eucharist.-

> Godhead here in hiding whom I do adore,
> Masked by these bare shadows, shape and nothing more;
> See, Lord at Thy service low here lies a heart
> Lost, all lost in wonder at the God Thou Art![2]

Shut Up and Get in Line

According to the Council of Trent, the Sacrifice of the altar, being substantially the same as that of Calvary, pleases God more than all the sins of this world displeases Him. (St. Thomas)

The Mass has infinite value and at each Mass, adoration, reparation and thanksgiving of limitless value are infallibly offered up to God.

"At the Consecration, a great surge of adoration rises up toward God and when that moment arrives, all is silent. This sacred silence tells what music cannot express. It is a silence that mirrors the silence which, according to the Apocalypse (8:1), occurred in Heaven when the Lamb opened the book of seven seals. May this silence of the Consecration be our solace and our strength.

The spirit of evil fears nothing so much as a Mass, especially one celebrated with great fervor and in which many souls participate with a spirit of faith. When the enemy of goodness meets some insurmountable obstacle, it is because in some church there was a priest, conscious of his own weakness and poverty, who with faith offered up the very powerful Host and Blood of our Redemption." (Taken from Our Savior and His Love for Us by Fr. Reginald Garrigou-Lagrange, O.P.)

There are so many miracles associated with the Holy Eucharist, and books documenting their authenticity. Saints have levitated, glowed, wept, and have gone into ecstasy when receiving Holy Communion. Consecrated Hosts have turned into actual Flesh and Consecrated wine has turned into Blood. God has given us these miracles that we may believe and be strengthened by that belief.

One of the most famous miracles which has been approved by the Church and science, proving the Real Presence of our Lord in the Eucharist, is the Miracle of Lanciano. At this Italian Shrine, a priest had doubted the Real Presence of our Lord in the Eucharist. During the Consecration of the Mass, the Sacred Host changed into Flesh from a Human Heart and the wine was changed into Human Blood. The miracle is still there for veneration and when pilgrims come to behold the Miracle of Lanciano, they are brought to their knees in tears.

When Pope John Paul II visited our country, security guards brought special search dogs into the cathedral where Our Holy Father would be celebrating Mass. There was no one in the cathedral at all, but when the dogs reached the altar, they barked continuously at the Tabernacle, which we know holds Our dear Lord and Savior in the Blessed Sacrament.

Even one miracle of a bleeding Host should be more than enough to get our attention, but there have been many instances of these miracles.

EWTN has a powerful video about Eucharistic Miracles. Mother Angelica said, "This video has been a tool to focus us on what really happens on the Altar and Who dwells in the Tabernacle."

Many of us have a genuine hunger for the Eucharist, but we don't really understand that is what we need. When a little child is hungry or tired, he knows something is wrong, but he can't understand, pinpoint or verbalize what he needs. So too, we are like little children that feel a need, a longing, a hunger for something greater than what we have. Saint John of the Cross calls it The Hole in the Soul. Only God can fill that void and we will not find peace or contentment until we rest in Him. Faith is fueled by our actions. We must first act and pray hard that we may believe, and then the actual gift will come. And what a gift it is, all for the asking! Saint Augustine explains this concept simply, yet brilliantly, "Faith is to believe what you do not see; the reward of this faith is to see what you believe."[3] Isaiah 7:9 clearly instructs us in this matter- "Believe that you may understand."

Saint Thomas Aquinas helps us put the beautiful gift of Faith into perspective; "To one who has faith, no explanation is necessary. To one without faith, no explanation is possible."[4]

Father Leo Clifford O.S.M. talks about Adoration on EWTN in a series called "Reflections." I love listening to him speak so inspiringly about Our Blessed Lord present in the Holy Eucharist. Father says, "There is no length, no depth to which our captive God will not go to be with us. And we, foolish, thoughtless children hurry on our busy streets and crowded theatres and go on our way unthinking, while the Divine Magnificence waits in the unvisited solitude of the Tabernacle."

Times spent in Holy Communion and Adoration are the most valuable and precious moments of our whole lives. St. Faustina so eloquently praises the Lord as she speaks of the miraculous Eucharist- "O King of Glory, though you hide your beauty, yet the eye of my soul rends the veil. I see the angelic choirs giving you honor without cease."

"Because God exists outside of time, the past, present and future are all spread out before Him, like a vast panorama. He sees them all, in one view."[5] Christ is the focal point in that panorama.

"Christ is the treasure, the pearl of great price, and the sanctuary lamp in every Catholic Church is the beacon light flickering this truth, so secret, so public, so mysterious, so simple."

These beautiful words were written in the 1950's on a holy card by an unidentified source. "We need but direct our footsteps to the door of the Catholic church and "enter the door as if the floor within were gold; and every wall of jewels all of wealth untold; as if a choir in robes of fire were singing here; not shout nor rush but hush...for God is here!"[6]

"It is said of St. Francis of Assisi that "every fiber of his heart was kindled into love for the Sacrament of Christ's Body," and he constantly urged his brothers to bring others to know and love Christ living in the Blessed Sacrament. From this love sprang St. Francis' deep reverence for priests. He declared that if he confronted with an angel and an unworthy priest, he would kiss the hand that had touched the Body of Christ before saluting the angel. One day someone pointed out a priest living in notorious sin. Francis instantly knelt before him, kissing his hands and saying, "These hands have touched my Lord, and out of love for Him I honor His vicar. For himself he may be bad; for me he is good."[7] The priest was overwhelmed with sorrow for his sins.

"Man should tremble, the world should vibrate, all Heaven should be deeply moved when the Son of God appears on the altar in the hands of the priest."
St. Francis of Assisi

"There is a school in Heaven and there one has only to learn how to love. The school is in the Cenacle, the Teacher is Jesus, The matter taught is His Flesh and His Blood."
St. Gemma Galgani

Chapter 32
"OFFENSIVE LINES"
Ninth Grade Bad Habits

After graduating from St. Joseph's Elementary School, I attended Bishop Conwell High School. One thing I missed from grade school were the times that were built into our schedule for the Lavatory. In high school, we had no time to visit the Ladies Room. We rushed from class to class and no one wanted to tell the teacher that she had "an emergency" and needed to go. By the end of the day, I couldn't wait until I got home "to go." After the bus left us off, my friend Clair and I walked a few streets until we went our separate ways. The problem was, by the time we were half way home, we got ourselves laughing so hard, one or both of us usually couldn't hold it in anymore. We laughed with convulsions at everything under the sun. There was a big rock on the way home. Whoever got to it first to sit down was usually the one who went home dry. The other poor soul was left standing, an unfortunate victim of her uncontrollable laughter. At this point, she would probably just sit on the grass, and well, - go. There we sat, two pathetic little swine who had lost complete control of their senses. At the time, I would never have guessed that Clair would grow up to be the refined owner of two Tea-Rooms and would teach proper etiquette to others.

My laughing habit became my downfall Freshman year. One day my mother had enough! The things she yelled seemed to be more appropriate for an immature four-year old, but they were directed at an undignified, fourteen-year old loser. "Ewww! What kind of a good catholic girl would come home to her family like this?!! How disgusting! You're a disgrace to the uniform! If you come home all p_ _sed one more time, you're staying in for the rest of the year!" She really meant it too! I knew we were gross, but it wasn't our fault. After having us on a bathroom schedule for eight years straight, we weren't the ones who changed things around. And if it was up to us, we would never have made the bus stops so far from our houses. Anyway, it's not like we did it on purpose. We were just laughing.

For a few days after that, I asked the cafeteria Moderator to be excused. That solved the problem temporarily, but the first day I forgot to ask, I was back to my old habit. This time, I knew I would get punished if I went home in my deplorable condition, so I decided to stop at my friend Babs' house. I knew she would help to figure out something. She always prided herself on her ability to beat the system. After hearing of my dilemma, Babs quietly walked over to the hall closet and took out an iron. I questioned her intention, "Don't you think we should wet it first?" Babs replied, "It's already wet, Stupid. Doesn't your mother want to see it dry?" Babs did relent a bit, though. She threw some Jean Nate perfume on the uniform while ironing it, all the while reassuring me, "You know the uniform is to be DRY cleaned only, because of the wool fabric." She also acknowledged that lots of girls at her school had this same problem. "Everybody's doing it," she said. "Every time we laugh, it happens. It can't be helped." Babs was popular at her school, so I felt great to be one of the In-Crowd! My mom was happy to see that I conquered my bad habit (no pun intended).

A few years later, Babs would take out her iron again. This time she

Shut Up and Get in Line

planned to iron my long curly hair until it was poker straight for my senior picture. The two of us knew that my new beautiful hairdo would cause a sensation. As she was telling me how gorgeous my hair would turn out, I thought I smelled smoke! I jumped up from under the ironing board and sure enough, my hair was scorched, ultra-thin and just short of catching fire! I was outraged! Babs examined the iron and remarked, "Oh look, it has a steam setting. Wanna try that?"

(I wasn't the only black sheep of the family. A few short months earlier, during exam week, an announcement came over the St. Joes P.A. System. "Whoever is throwing up every day in the Playground, better report to the school nurse immediately!!" The identity of that vile creature was never discovered by the school authorities, but it was none other than that red-head, freckle-faced little brother of mine, Jerry. We weren't the classiest family in the Parish.)

In ninth grade, our Study Hall was held in the gym. One of the first few weeks of high school, I was hard at work on the bleachers when the girl sitting next to me was involved in a skirmish! She was innocently studying and minding her own business when a person who was under the bleachers tried to take her shoe! What in the world?! The girl quietly wrestled for her shoe and won it back, but the whole incident launched me into a fit of laughter from which I was not recovering. The scene repeated itself a few moments later- new girl, new shoe, but the same quiet, hilarious struggle.

I wondered who these runaway clowns were, and how can I get down there with them? I longed to be part of this new and inviting underground world where all the fun was happening! When the bell rang I recognized one of the girls under the bleachers. She was Maggie, a girl who I knew from grade school. Maggie was very funny and daring. The next day I was right down in the muck with her under the bleachers. It was now my turn to grab the shoe of some poor unsuspecting girl and laugh my fool head off. I spotted an easy target and started to pull the shoe, but the dizzy owner of the shoe went ape and carried on, "Sister, help! Sister, help!" How could this crackpot do this to me??? What's wrong with people, anyway? Why can't they just do the right thing? No one got Maggie in trouble yesterday! Isn't there some kind of unwritten code about protecting those who are entertaining the class? She was just supposed to laugh quietly and I would have given her shoe back. She didn't have to make a big scene and act like she was dying! Ugh - some people will do anything for attention! Did she think that I wanted to keep her scurvy old shoe? I already had two ugly saddle shoes just like hers and every other kid in the school.

The Discipline Office happened to be right across the hall from the gym and Mother Gabriella, the Disciplinarian was summoned to the scene of the crime. Mother positioned herself at the opening of the bleachers. Her instructions were LOUD and CLEAR! "Come on out girls and pick up your Detention Slips!"

Mother was not happy with us. I felt completely lame and worthless. At home, another mother would be even more disappointed. My sister, a senior, was earning exceptional grades as a model student while I was busy dragging our good name through the mud.

Chapter 33

"LINE OF ACTION"
A Few Catholics Who Shared Their Faith

There are millions of Catholics sharing their faith with others who have benefited from having known a Priest or Sister during the course of their lifetime. Here are a few famous ones.

"King of the One Liners" – Bob Hope

Bob Hope brought such joy and humor to others that some called him "a national treasure." He gave of himself unselfishly to entertain at camps and bases all over the world, bringing laughter and cheer to our military men when they needed it most. He also was a generous philanthropist who shared his gifts and wealth with so many others.

"During World War II, when Cardinal Spellman was not only the Archbishop of New York, but also the Bishop for the men and women in the Military Services, he and Bob would often meet at army camps and overseas bases. They developed a friendly and joking relationship. For example, when Bob told the Cardinal that he had been so tired that he fell asleep during His Eminence's Midnight Mass homily, the Cardinal replied that it was perfectly alright since he often slept through Bob's monologues.

Bob was often associated with Catholic projects, often in partnership with his beautiful wife, Dolores, a devout Catholic. One such endeavor was the Our Lady of Hope Chapel at the Basilica of the National Shrine of the Immaculate Conception in Washington, made possible by contributions from the couple.

Bob was received into the Catholic Church in 1996 without fanfare because it was a very personal thing."[1] May Bob find all the happiness, joy and laughter in Heaven that he gave to us here on earth. Thanks for the memories, Bob.

"The Wanderer gets back in Line" - Dion

Does anybody here remember our talented brother, Dion? Of course you do! He had so many wonderful hits that he was inducted into the Rock and Roll Hall of Fame. Here are just a few, "I Wonder Why," "Teenager in Love," "Run Around Sue," "Where or When," "The Wanderer," "Abraham, Martin and John."

I remember in sixth grade being in a Halloween dance contest. We were dancing to "Runaround Sue." When I was a music teacher, I had my students listen to Dion's song, "Abraham, Martin and John." Then they wrote about it in their music journals and drew pictures. Some of their sentiments were so beautiful and touching that I wanted to cry.

Dion said that when he was a boy growing up in the Bronx, a priest- (now a Bishop,) named Monsignor Peneconni stood outside the church and drilled into Dion's head sayings about the virtues, good character and the soul. Dion said that the Monsignor was so relentless in his attempt to instill these important truths into the young boy's head. Monsignor told Dion that a virtuous man is a happy man and that virtue was "a habitual and firm disposition to do the good." He did not understand Monsignor's message at the time, but those words never left his head.

After selling millions of records and making millions of dollars, Dion was caught up in the world of adulation, alcohol and drugs. His wife, Susan helped him through his darkest days. Dion knew at the center of his being that something was wrong. He tried different denominations but they were always missing something and incomplete. Dion remembered Monsignor's lessons to him when he needed them most. "In his own words on his official website www.diondimucci.com, Dion states, "Now I know what I was missing. It's the Eucharist, the fullness of faith, the Communion of Saints, the beauty of truth. I was missing two thousand years of family history and rich tradition." Dion, with all his millions recognized the truth and came back home where he belonged. He returned to his boyhood church, Mount Carmel Catholic Church where it all began. He went to Confession and Father stretched out his arms and said to that Wanderer, "Welcome Home, Dion."[2]

(There is something to be said about returning to the church where you had first received Holy Communion. Every time I return to Saint Joes where I received my Sacraments, I never fail to have a powerful spiritual experience. I think it's because that is the place where I first was united with Jesus as a child. It's like going back to be with an old friend at your special spot (but of course, even better). I would encourage anyone who ever has the opportunity to visit the church where you made your First Holy Communion, to do so and I think you will return again and again.)

"Full of Grace"- Guidelines for Women – Johnette Benkovic

Johnette Benkovic, who began the Women of Grace meetings in the churches across America, is creating nothing short of a Feminine Revolution, (not to be confused with the radical feminist movement of the sixties). Using the informative "Full of Grace" books and video tapes with Johnette doing the teaching, women are brought together in their own parishes to learn and grow in the faith. Using the perfect woman, Our Blessed Mother as their role model, women are reminded of their authentic femininity, their gift of mothering and nurturing everyone who is put in their path. Through sharing together, their souls are healed from past mistakes and sufferings. The lies of the radical feminist movement are exposed along with the harmful effects of their "free love" philosophy. The physical, spiritual and emotional dangers and scars of birth control and abortion are brought to light.

Johnette hosts the excellent Catholic call- in radio show, Moments of Truth, with Father Ed Sylvia.

Johnette said that her grandmother prayed a Rosary for each of her thirteen grandchildren every day. She called the Rosary 'Our Lady's Lasso.' Needless to say, Our Lady's Lasso must have pulled Johnette back to the Church after falling away for a time, and greatly helped in her important church ministry.

Shut Up and Get in Line

"Famous Hollywood Headliner Meets Fatima's Sister Lucia"

– Mel Gibson

"During the filming of "The Passion," each day began with Confessions and the celebration of Mass. Both Mel Gibson and Jim Caviziel, the actor who plays Jesus, pray the Rosary.

According to Mr. Richard Salbato of the Fatima based Unity Publishing Co., Mel Gibson had come to Fatima in September, 2003 to ask Our Lady's help on the film. After pondering the subject of our Lord's Passion for over a decade, Mel Gibson put the project in Our Lady's hands. This is why "The Passion of Christ" is unique, unlike any other "Jesus film" before or since.

"The Passion" is based on biblical and historical facts. Mr. Gibson also was inspired by writings of two holy, catholic nuns, the Diaries of Sister Anne Catherine Emmerich and Mary of Agreda's "The City of God."

As for Mr. Gibson's visit with Sister Lucia, who spoke with the Virgin Mary in Fatima, Portugal in 1917, the last living Fatima visionary- Imagine the honor of meeting someone who actually saw and conversed with the Queen of Heaven, someone who saw the Mother of God in all her beauty and glory. Was this meeting with Sister Lucia a gift from Our Lady to Mr. Gibson for the manner in which he used his artistic talents to honor the sufferings of her Divine Son? I wouldn't doubt it for a minute!"[3]

"Come and see the tents of the soldiers of Christ. Come and see their order of battle; they fight every day and every day defeat and immolate the passions that assail us."

St. John Chrysostom

Chapter 34

"WHAT'S MY LINE?"
Choose Your Service

We are all commissioned by our Lord to go out and make disciples of all nations Matt.28:19-20. Are we doing our part in bringing the Good News of Jesus to others? What line of work are we involved with in the church?

As brothers and sisters, we must look after one another. Is there someone hurting that we could help? Is there a kind act we could do for another child of God? There are countless lonely, broken-hearted, abused or neglected children, the sick, the widows, the orphans, the imprisoned and the helpless unborn. Where can our Lord use you to bring His love to one of His children?

Saint Basil the Great reminds us to share our gifts with others- "The bread you store up belongs to the hungry; the cloak that lies in your chest belongs to the naked; the gold that you have hidden in the ground belongs to the poor."[1]

Saint Teresa of Avila encourages us to step up and use ourselves to help lighten the burden of another:

"Christ has no body on earth but yours, no hands but yours, no feet but yours. Yours are the eyes through which Christ's compassion for the world is to look out; yours are the feet with which He is to go about doing good; and yours are the hands with which He is to bless us now."[2]

Chapter 35

"A REWARDING LINE OF WORK"
Religious Life

At this time in history, our faith continues to be under attack and ridicule. We know that the Church "will stand until the end of time and the gates of hell will not prevail against it." We must remember the special significance and supreme importance of our beautiful Catholic faith and the special souls our Lord used to teach that faith to us. God used them in a mighty way to help us to understand that by walking along the straight and narrow path, the shortest distance between earth and Heaven, we have a direct line to our final and eternal destination.

Religious life is very rewarding, yet full of temptations. St. John Chrysostom in "Contemplations on the Priesthood," gives us an idea of the evil that lies in waiting and wants to crush our Priests every day. "I know my own soul, how feeble and puny it is. I know the magnitude of the ministry and the great difficulty of the work; for more stormy billows vex the soul of the Priest than the gales which disturb the sea."

Shut Up and Get in Line

This is how I picture God talking to His priests and nuns:

"A CALL TO MY ARMS"

"Mother Teresa," said a voice from above,
"My children need your tender love.
Will you care for the sick as they deserve?"
Mother said, "Yes, Lord, I will serve."

"Father Groeschel," the Lord said one day,
"My little ones need to hear what you say.
Will you write and speak and help them now?"
Father replied, "Yes, Lord, I shall."

"Mother Angelica," spoke the Lord from His throne,
"I need you to speak out and make My ways known
Begin a worldwide network, Will you start today?"
Mother said, "Lord, I will obey."

"Father Conrad," God said from on High,
"The whole universe trembles when My babies die.
Defend life and tell them never to kill."
Father responded, "Yes Lord, I will."

"Father Corapi," he heard the Lord say,
"Use your strong, bold voice to teach and pray.
Will you travel the world and proclaim what you know?"
Father said, "Yes, Lord, I will go."

"All My Priests and Nuns, wherever you are
The whole world over, near or far,
You are My beloved. You have answered My call,
You are close to My heart, each one and all.

I planted a seed in the depths of your soul,
You responded with Joy to your beautiful role.
My glorious purpose for the life of each one
Is to win souls for Heaven in the Name of My Son.

You have sacrificed all because you love Me,
You are martyred and mocked by those who don't see.
Work in My vineyards of missions and schools,
Tend to My flock and teach them My rules.

Shut Up and Get in Line

Feed My poor children and hug them for Me,
Use your gifts for the orphans and widows you see.
Pray for My infants who are swept to their death
Even before they take their first breath.

Care for the sick in sorrow and strife,
You have promised to serve all the days of your life.
Should you fall in this good and evil War,
Step back on the path that leads to My door.

My heart with an ocean of Mercy will flood
And transform the whole world with My Body and Blood
If you give Me yourselves, My special ones,
I will give you Heaven, My Priests and My Nuns.

"Labor on 'til I call you home with Me,
And you will rest in My Arms for eternity.
Will you do all these things and love Me still?"
They answered in chorus, "Yes, Lord, we will."

Chapter 36

"DROPPING JAWLINES"
Out of the Mouths of First Grade Babies

As a teacher, I experienced some of what the good sisters endured with us. Children sometimes say and do the most bizarre and unbelievable things. I often felt like an idiot in my classroom laughing uncontrollably at some of the incredible things that came out of the "mouths of babes." Tears rolled down my cheeks many times during the special days that I was blessed to spend with children. I will just recant one incident here.

One day while my first graders were taking a test, I was working at my desk. Michael, a self-appointed little helper appeared at my desk and said, "Miss Moore, Greg picked his nose and put it on the desk." Disgusted and weak-stomached, I did not want to be involved in this gross occurrence. I looked up at Michael and quietly instructed him, "Tell Greg To Get It Off The Desk!" I couldn't watch. I was already gagging. Michael returned to me a few moments later and proudly announced. "It's all taken care of, Miss Moore. I made Greg put it back in his nose."

Chapter 37

"ARE YOU NEXT IN LINE?"
Don't Get Ready, Be Ready!

At this very moment in time, we are standing in line to be judged. Imagine all the people who lived before us, all of the people who are alive now and all the ones who will come after us- in a long line. We are all moving up the line towards the Judgment Seat. Someday, it will be our turn to cross over from our earthly home into our eternal home. One at a time, we are edging closer to our final destiny and our turn to be judged. The interesting and sobering fact is that we do not know where we are standing in that line. Will it be our turn to cross over tonight, tomorrow or perhaps in twenty years?

Is it worth stepping off the straight and narrow path and living our life out of sync, out of line with what we know is God's will? Will we chance doing things our own way and put our eternal salvation at stake? If we are called home this very day, are we prepared to meet our Maker or will we be ashamed of ourselves and afraid to see Him?

The thought of Eternity must be constantly in our thoughts.

At the present moment, are you living your life in alignment with the Laws of God?

There are so many books written about God's love and the beauty of Heaven, and they are beautiful, but that's just the half of it. God's

Justice is as real as His love. The honest reality is that Hell is just as real as Heaven, and like Heaven, is eternal.

Consider these earnest and no nonsense warnings from one of our great moral theologians and Doctors of the church, St. Alphonsus Liguouri:

"It is certain that hell is a pit of fire, in which the miserable souls of the wicked will be tormented forever. Even in this life the pain of burning is of all pains the most intense and dreadful; but the fire of hell has the power of inflicting much more excruciating torment, because it has been created by God to be the instrument of his wrath upon his rebellious creatures. "Go, ye cursed, into everlasting fire," is the sentence of the reprobate. And as in this sentence of condemnation fire is particularly mentioned, we may conclude that, of all the torments with which the senses of the wicked are afflicted, fire is the greatest.

Ah, my God, for how many years past have I deserved to burn in this fire! But Thou has waited for me, to behold me burning, not with this dreadful fire, but with the blessed flames of Thy holy love, Wherefore do I love Thee, my sovereign good, and desire to love Thee forever.

In this world fire burns only outwardly, and does not penetrate our interior; but in hell the fire enters into the inmost recesses of its victims. "Thou shalt make them as an oven of fire." Everyone will become as a furnace of fire, so that the heart will burn within the chest, the bowels within the carcass, the brains within the skull, and even the marrow within the bones. Sinners, what are your feelings with regard to this fire? You, who cannot now bear a spark accidentally fallen from a candle, nor a house too hot, nor a ray of the sun upon your head, how will you endure to be permanently immersed in an ocean of fire, where

Shut Up and Get in Line

you will be forever dying, and yet, never die?

With the devouring fire, the gloom which darkens; the cries of the damned which deafen; the stench, which would be enough to cause those miserable beings to die, if die they could; the closeness which oppresses and hinders their breath; the bitterest subject of their wailing is the thought that, through their own fault, they have lost God."[1]

Yikes!! That's one place to avoid at all costs! Sometimes we need a good shove from one of our strong older brothers to push us back in line.

We need to keep the goal line before us and be prepared without an instants notice to cross that line and account for every second which we were given on earth. Inherent in each immortal soul is a conscience complete with all the means necessary to reach our Heavenly Homeland. We were told that we would not be left orphans, but were given food for the journey, the Bread of Life in the Holy Eucharist. We were also given the Bible, a letter written from Home from our Heavenly Father with all the directions we need, if we only would follow them.

To ignore God and His Commandments is tantamount to playing with fire. You could be next in line. If He does call you home today, will He say, "Well done, good and faithful servant, now enter into My glory?" or "Be cursed, I never knew you." Don't chance it. You may be closer than you think to the front of the line.

> "My Lord, if it is necessary to give them a whipping or
> two to convert them, please do it as long as their souls
> are saved in the end."
>
> Padre Pio of Pietrelcina

Chapter 38

"RUN STRAIGHT FOR THE GOAL LINE"
Focus, Perseverance, Victory

There are many pitfalls on the road we must travel to claim our family inheritance. Dangerous and deadly temptations abound, waiting and wanting to push us off the straight and narrow path. Be constantly vigilant and on guard. Remember the importance of family loyalty and protect your family's good name. Many of us struggle daily with sins against all the commandments. We must overcome Greed, Cursing, Disobedience, Anxiety, Anger, Fighting, Lying, Envy, Sloth, Lust, Gluttony, Presumption, Despair, Pride, Drunkenness, Stealing.

Saint Dominic said, "A man who governs his passions is master of the world. We must either command them, or be commanded by them. It is better to be a hammer than an anvil."[1] Saint Gregory of Nyssa warns us," Anger, fear, cowardice, arrogance, pleasure, grief, hatred, spite, heartless cruelty, jealousy, flattery, bearing grudges and resentment, and all the other hostile drives within us; There is your array of the masters, and tyrants that try to enslave the soul, their prisoner of war, and bring it under their control."[2]

I had a nun once who drew a straight vertical line on the board with an arrow pointing up. She drew a stick figure on the line and said it represented us on our way up to heaven. Then she erased the stick figure from the line and placed it next to the line on its side. Sister said this represents us when we sin and fall off the path that leads to heaven. She told us how important it was for us to get right back on the right path. "Do not stay there!" Sister said, "Get right back on the path that will take you to heaven!" These types of images are powerful to children and stay with them their whole lives. Thank God.

The nuns and priests left nothing to chance. They persisted in teaching us the complete truth and they didn't pull any punches. I miss the nuns and priests of my youth.

How many of us would have been better off later in life, if a nun would have shown up to pull us off of a bar stool and used the pointer to show us the door? I could have used a nun popping in to admonish me when I needed it- "Catherine, put that spoon down! How many hot fudge sundaes can one person possibly consume?!"

Wouldn't we have benefited from encountering the authoritative figure of a priest on our wayward journey to some indiscretion? How many times did we get sucked into gossiping about our neighbor? I would have greatly profited if a good nun were there to yell at me-"SILENCE!"

We can sometimes still hear faint reminders in our heads about how we should conduct ourselves; "Stand up straight!" or "Tuck in that shirt tail!"

I think the order, "Shut up and get in line!" is way too mild for some of us. We could have used harsher directions, like- "Catherine, shut your big judgmental mouth and get your lazy little butt in line!" I am still learning to shut up and just stop talking,- learning to listen and be still, peaceful, patient, and conform. As far as getting in line, I'm still struggling to keep focused on eternal things, take the high road, following all of God's Laws and not stray from the straight and narrow path.

Silence really is golden. It's when we can hear God speaking to us. Saint Faustina once asked the Lord why He doesn't speak to His people anymore and He replied, "I do, but with all the noise of the world, they can't hear Me."

The nuns tried to teach us the huge value of silence years ago and it always went something like this:

Sister: "Catherine, were you talking?"
Me: "Stir, I just said…
Sister: "Ut"
Me: "All I said was…
Sister: "Ut"
Me: "I didn't…
Sister: "Ut?"
Me: "But I…
Sister: "Ut!"
Me: "But…
Sister: "Ut?"
Me: "Yes, Stir."

In the book, "Conformity to God's Will," St. Alphonsus Liguori writes:

The devout Father John Tauler relates this personal experience: For years he had prayed God to send him someone who would teach him the real spiritual life. One day, at prayer, he heard a voice saying, "Go to such and such a church and you will have the answer to your prayers." He went and at the door of the church he found a beggar, barefooted and

Shut Up and Get in Line

in rags. He greeted the mendicant saying: "Good day, my friend."

"Thank you, sir, for your kind wishes, but I do not recall ever having had a 'bad' day."

"Then God has certainly given you a very happy life."

"That is very true, sir. I have never been unhappy. In saying this I am not making any rash statement either. This is the reason: when I have nothing to eat, I give thanks to God; when it rains or snows, I bless God's providence; when someone insults me, drives me away, or otherwise mistreats me, I give glory to God. I said I've never had an unhappy day, and it's the truth, because I am accustomed to will unreservedly what God wills. Whatever happens to me, sweet or bitter, I gladly receive from His hands as what is best for me. Hence my unvarying happiness."

"Where did you find God?"

"I found him where I left creatures."

"Who are you anyway?"

"I am a king."

"And where is your kingdom?"

"In my soul where everything is in good order, where the passions obey reason, and reason obeys God."

"How have you come to such a state of perfection?"

"By silence, I practice silence towards men, while I cultivate the habit of speaking with God. Conversing with God is the way I found and maintain my peace of soul."

Union with God brought this poor beggar to the very heights of perfection. In his poverty he was richer than the mightiest monarch, in his sufferings, he was vastly happier than worldlings amid their worldly delights."[3]

So, it looks like the nuns and priests had it right all along. They gave their all in trying to prepare us for life in this world and the next. They did their part in assisting our parents to raise good and faithful boys and girls. As special helpers chosen by God Himself and called into His service, they taught us how fleeting is this world and how everlasting is the next.

Sooner or later, with God's grace, all the important and inspiring lessons we were taught as children will sink in. Thank God the good old Catholic guilt awakens something in our conscience and nags us until we come home to the truth where we belong.

The nuns and priests (to use one of my dad's expressions) "got a bum rap."

Yes, they were strict, but we needed them to be strict. And if they were harsh sometimes, so what! When I think of the things that have issued forth from my mouth as an adult, it would make the poor nuns blush.

In an age when priests and nuns are being criticized, disrespected and mistrusted, we must remember Who chose them and Who their Boss is. We need to be grateful for our nuns and priests and thank them for teaching us all the important things in life.

There are those who say that they are leaving the Church because of scandal. Whose dirty little hand will pick up the first stone to hurl at a fallen priest, nun, or anyone else? That's not our job. Everyone is a sinner and we must never leave our Lord and Savior because one of His servants has sinned. You would never leave your parents and go running out to live in a stranger's house because one of your brothers or sisters did something bad. In the same way, do not abandon Christ and the true Church because some of our brothers and sisters have fallen. Rather, we should help them up. We need to pray for them just as others have prayed for us over the years when we needed it most. There is no sin too great for God's mercy and God forgives us all when we're sorry. In an instant our Lord can take the biggest sinner and make him the greatest Saint. If we are forgiving to others, God will forgive us. He reminded us of this truth on the Sermon on the Mount, "Blessed are the merciful, for they will obtain mercy."[4]

Always remain loyal to Holy Mother Church and remember the words of Saint Boniface, "The Church is like a great ship being pounded by the waves of life's different stresses. Our duty is not to abandon ship, but to keep her on her course."[5]

> "I think that if God forgives us, we must forgive ourselves. Otherwise it is almost like setting up ourselves as a higher tribunal than Him."
>
> C.S.Lewis

Many times we think we are the judge and jury of another, but there is only one Judge and someday we will each stand before Him.

This old poem is lovely and we can all identify with The Child on the Judgment Seat

"THE CHILD ON THE JUDGMENT SEAT"

Where hast been toiling all day, sweetheart,
That thy brow is burdened and sad?
The Master's work may make weary feet,
But it leaves the spirit glad.

Was thy garden nipped with the midnight frost,
Or scorched with the midday glare?
Were thy vines laid low, or thy lilies crushed,
That thy face is so full of care?

"No pleasant garden toils were mine!
I have sat on the judgment seat,
Where the Master sits at eve, and calls
The children around his feet."

How camest thou on the judgment seat,
Sweetheart? Who set thee there?
"Tis a lonely and lofty seat for thee,
And well might fill thee with care.

Shut Up and Get in Line

"I climbed on the judgment seat myself;
I have sat there alone all day;
For it grieved me to see the children around
Idling their life away."

"They wasted the Master's precious seed,
They wasted the precious hours;
They trained not the vines, nor gathered the fruits,
And they trampled the sweet, meek flowers."

And what hast thou done in the Judgment seat, Sweetheart?
What didst thou there?
Would the idlers heed thy childish voice?
Did the garden mend by thy care?

"Nay, that grieved me more! I called and cried,
But they left me there forlorn;
My voice was weak, and they heeded not,
Or they laughed my words to scorn."

Ah, the judgment seat was not for thee!
The servants were not thine!
And the Eyes which adjudge the praise and the blame,
See further than thine or mine.

The Voice that shall sound there at eve, sweetheart,
Will not raise its tones to be heard:
It will hush the earth, and hush the hearts,
And none will resist its word.

"Should I see the Master's treasures lost,
The stores that should feed his poor,
And not lift my voice, be it weak as it may,
And not be grieved sore?"

Wait till the evening falls, sweetheart,
Wait till the evening falls;
The Master is near, and knoweth all:
Wait till the Master calls.

But how fared thy garden plot, sweetheart,
Whilst thou sat on the judgment seat?
Who watered thy roses, and trained thy vines,
And kept them from careless feet?

"Nay, that is saddest of all to me!
That is saddest of all!
My vines are trailing, my roses are parched,
My lilies droop and fall."

Go back to thy garden plot, sweetheart,
Go back till the evening falls;

Shut Up and Get in Line

And bind thy lilies, and train thy vines,
Till for thee the Master calls.

Go make thy garden fair as thou canst-
Thou workest never alone;
Perchance he whose plot is next to thine
Will see it, and mend his own.

And the next may copy his, sweetheart,
Till all grows fair and sweet;
And, when the Master comes at eve,
Happy faces his coming will greet.

Then shall thy joy be full, sweetheart,
In the garden so fair to see,
In the Master's words of praise for all,
In a look of his own for thee.

Elizabeth Rundle Charles[6]

My mother always told me, "Tend to your own knittin." Like the child on the judgment seat, whenever we spend our time criticizing our neighbor's lives, we are neglecting our own work. These enlightening words from Saint John of the Cross can greatly help us in getting our judging problems under control. "Don't think that, because the particular virtues you have in mind don't shine in your neighbor, he won't be precious in God's sight for something you're not thinking about."[7]

Eventually, we must stand alone, without the help and guidance of our parents, sisters, teachers or priests. We must remember to live the Christ-centered life for which we were trained. When our Divine Master calls us home, we need to stand with confidence that we had done all in our power to love, obey and conform to His plan for us.

Saint Cyprian said, "The Divine Mercy is an inexhaustible fountain. They who bring vessels of the greatest confidence, draw from it the greatest graces."

The Bible tells us in Esdras 5:42, "He answered them, "the Final Judgment can be compared to a circle, and just as a circle has no beginning or end; so those who come early will not be too early and those who come late will not be too late."

We are all waiting in the Judgment Line right now. We may be just steps away from entering our eternal home, for the better or the worse. When will we cross over the line and take our spot before the Judgment Seat?

Chapter 39

"CONNECTING LINES"
Jacob's Ladder

"He dreamed that he saw a stairway reaching from earth to Heaven, with angels going up and coming down from it."

Genesis 28-12

"Jacob's Ladder" ... is a faithful representation of the devout life. The two sides between which we ascend, and which support the steps, are prayer, which bring the love of God, and the Sacraments that confer it. The steps are but the various degrees of charity by which we advance from virtue to virtue, either descending in action to the aid of our neighbor, or ascending in contemplation to a loving union with God." (St. Francis de Sales)[1]

- How will we use the lines in our lives? To box ourselves in and stay prisoners to our own shallow passions?
- Will we cut ourselves off from God's desire for our happiness or will we stay open and obedient to His Divine Will?
- Will we build bridges instead of fences, extend ourselves and be willing to be a living, breathing example of Christ's love?
- Will we pick up our cross and follow in His bloody footprints to our

Heavenly destiny?
- Will we use the straight line, the shortest distance between two points, to get from earth to Heaven, or will we step off the straight and narrow path and leave our salvation to chance?
- Will we make use of the precious Body and Blood of Jesus as our life line?
- Will we examine our conscience in the Confession Line? Can we feel the family ties between all of our brothers and sisters in the Communion Line?
- Will we break Satan's chains of bondage as he tempts us to sin, hiding behind enemy lines?
- Will we stand firm, courageous and resolute on the front lines of battle between good and evil?
- When we reach the finish line, will we be welcomed home with open arms?

"Oh late have I known Thee, late have I loved Thee, Beauty ever Ancient and ever New!"[2]

Saint Augustine

"When the Sisters are exhausted, up to their eyes in work, when all seems to go awry, they spend an hour in prayer before the Blessed Sacrament. This practice has never failed to bear fruit; they experience peace and strength."

Blessed Mother Teresa

There are many things written about Purgatory. Some saints depict it as a terrible place, while others say the opposite. Saint Catherine of Genoa claimed that "There is no joy other than that in Paradise to be compared to the joy of the souls in Purgatory."

Father Benedict Groeschel wrote the Introduction of a book, The Dream of Gerontius, by Saint John Henry Newman. It is an exceptional poem which describes the death of an old man and his journey to the judgment seat of God.

Saint John Newman applies Saint Catherine's teaching to the experience of the man from the moment of death until his entrance into Purgatory. His Guardian Angel accompanies him into the purifying bath of Purgatory.

This is so beautiful and represents only a few verses of this touching poem:

THE DREAM OF GERONTIUS

The angel says to him-
"Softly and gently, dearly-ransomed soul,
In my most loving arms I now enfold thee,
And o'r the penal waters, as they roll,
I poise thee, and lower thee, and hold thee.
And carefully I dip thee in the lake,
And thou without a sob or resistance,
Dost through the flood thy rapid passage take,
Sinking deep, deeper into the dim distance.
Angels, to whom the willing task is given,

Shall tend and nurse, and lull thee, as thou liest,
And Masses on the earth and prayers
Shall aid thee at the throne of the Most Highest.
Farewell, but not forever! Brother dear,
Be brave and patient on thy bed of sorrow,
Swiftly shall pass the night of trial here,
And I will come and wake thee on the morrow."

Chapter 40

"LINING UP TO SAY THANK YOU"
Student Testimonies

Priests and Sisters have greatly impacted the lives of countless students. Here is a sample of actual testimonies given by former students of Conwell-Egan High School. These comments were taken from the twentieth and twenty-fifth high school Reunion souvenir books of the graduating class of 1969.

Sister M. Thaddeus
"Kind, thoughtful and encouraging to her students." Sharon B.

Sister Louise Marie
"She made learning a pleasure" Vivian G.M.

Father Pius
"Instilled the belief in me that I could make it in college and later on in life." John M.

Father Girard
"Greatest motivator for my career." John R.
"Inspired me to teach-presided at my wedding." Terrence B.

Sister Miriam DeLourdes, Sister Michael Eileen, Mother Gabriella
"They all let you see that nuns were human also and they really cared for us all." Theresa K.

Father Blandon
"Enthusiastic, in control and firm." Hugh M.
"Funny, tough guy." Tom C.

Father Andre
"One of the most caring individuals I've ever met." John G.

Father Pavlock
"Woke up my creativity." Thomas J.

Father Bonaventure
"Taught respect for others." Robert W.
"He would save quotations that he thought were neat…now I do that." Dan F.

Sister John Casimiri
"Very honest, open-minded and very caring of her students." Denise F.

Sister Camilla
"I can still remember the fear of going into her classroom. It was a class I was always prepared for. I guess Sister Camilla's tough but terrific teaching methods were the reasons I achieved the highest freshman Algebra average that year." Ann K.

Shut Up and Get in Line

Father Cletus Watson
"He was genuine, sensitive, understanding. He could relate to the students and you could tell that he liked the students and wasn't just putting up a front.-He officiated at our wedding." James N.

Father Stanley
"He was genuine." Deborah M.
"He must have been a saint to put up with us, especially MJG."

Father Sixtus
"Inspirational" Gregory S.

Father Pius
"Great sense of humor- Taught that learning could be fun even if you hated the subject." Paul F.

Father Wilfred
"Saw so much of him in the Discipline Office- tough but fair and caring underneath- strong right hook." Thomas N.

Father Isadore
"Genuinely interested in his students." Paul M.

Father Camilus, Father Vernon, Father Cletus
"All truly unique individuals." Dennis B.

Father Isadore
"Knew and taught material, never lost his cool." Mike G.

Sister Neomesia
"She always taught us something for life." Mary M.W.

Father Simon
"He was kind, understanding and funny and so entertaining." Mary D.S.

These favorite memories were also recalled by the same class of students:

"Couldn't remember the Alma Mater when I was inducted into the National Honor Society." John R.

"Getting my head stuck in a locker." Dennis O.

"Playing Father Wilfred in Blue-Gray Day Skit, then facing him in costume." John G.

"Every day was a rip-roaring adventure." Susan E.D.

"Watching Dennis O. get caught climbing to the roof while we were playing Man-Hunt during study hall." Frank M.S.

"Passing Spanish with a thirty-seven average." Danny C.

"Ned A. being dragged out of Assembly by Father Boneventure after nearly punching someone out. He got a double zero that day." Mike M.

Shut Up and Get in Line

"If there should ever be a monastery without a troublesome and bad-tempered member, it would be necessary to find one and pay him his weight in gold because of the great profit that results from this trial, when good use is made of it."

St. Bernard of Clairvaux

Chapter 41

"BROKEN LINES OF COMMUNICATION"
A Bad Confession

During my freshman year at Bishop Conwell High School the building was overcrowded because the boys hadn't yet moved to their new school, Bishop Egan. Some of the classes were held on the stage in the auditorium. My cousin, Patty, approached me one day and said, "I heard that someone on the stage swung across the desks on a rope when the teacher was writing on the board. I just knew it was you!"

Well, that Wacko wasn't me, but I was never so flattered that people would think so highly of me! I felt ten feet tall and really thought I had reached the pinnacle of success and was being recognized for my great courage.

After college, my life seemed to be one continuous ten year party. Even so, I still wanted to remain in the church, but I wanted to be in control and make my own rules. I thought I found the perfect solution of staying connected to the church at the Shrine of Our Lady of Czestochowa. There I found that the Polish priests had thick accents and I thought they would not be able to understand my sins in Confession. I knew I could get my sins forgiven and I wouldn't have to deal with the embarrassment in the telling of them. Talk about piling one sin on top of another. For years I carried on my deliberate deceitfulness, but through the humble countenance of the beautiful Polish priests, I eventually came to know what a despicable habit I had formed.

It wasn't until later, after learning more about their speech patterns that I realized that the priests had understood me all along.

Chapter 42

"CROSSING THE FINISH LINE"
Out of This World Family Reunion

Better not get too comfortable here. We're not staying that long. As adoptive children bound together through Baptism, we are the heirs to the magnificent royal dynasty. While still in exile, our hearts long to reach the safety of home and the welcoming arms of our perfect Father. When our sojourn on this earth ends, we will cross over the line to the last home we will ever have, and there we will remain for all time. The goal line is fast approaching. A grand family reunion awaits when we reach the ethereal realm of unimaginable treasures. At home with our Beloved Divine Family, Father, Son and Holy Spirit, we will rejoice in ecstasy with all of our devoted relatives, the loyal family of God. We can only imagine our divine inheritance, miraculous joy and breathtaking beauty of our eternal home. The sublime essence and awesome wonder of the Blessed Trinity will transcend our love, peace and laughter to new and extraordinary depths and heights that we cannot yet comprehend. We will finally join the symphony of angels and saints and the celestial orchestra singing in harmonious strands and playing on the heavenly instruments exquisite musical melodies, shining, yet dull in the shadow of our gleaming and resplendent Lord and Savior.

A glimpse of this ravishing love is given to us in the glorious gift of the Holy Eucharist, our Heavenly King Himself. With frequent

Shut Up and Get in Line

reception of this most splendid of all masterpieces, we begin to experience our Heavenly reward right in the here and now. So, we must keep in mind our final end and the only two choices that will be left, Heaven and Hell. As we move closer to the day when everything is put on the line and our final destiny is decided, we must keep eternity as our top priority.

One day we will stand before the Just Judge all alone. There, we will not be making any excuses- "Well, they were mean to me first," or "I screamed back at him because he screamed first." What excellent training we had to get us ready for when we stand before the Judgment Seat. Our parents, nuns and priests never let us stand there and make excuses for our poor behavior, and we certainly won't be able to make excuses on that day. God bless them for knowing how to shut us up and not accept our excuses or explanations for why we couldn't close our big mouths. God Bless them for making sure we walked in our straight lines. They knew this life was just a short preparation for the next and they rehearsed us well for the last line in which we will ever stand. God Bless them for their steadfast faith and sticking to the unwavering truth which they learned well and were passing onto us.

> "Train up a child in the way he should go, And when he is old he will not depart from it."
>
> Proverbs 22:6

May our Heavenly Father pour out his blessings abundantly on His special soldiers on this earth who fought valiantly in this spiritual battle for the Kingdom, the Power and the Glory of Almighty God. We can't get ready, we need to be ready.

Saint Paul encourages us to become spiritually mature and keep our attention on the finish line.

> "Brothers, I do not think of myself as having reached the finish line. I give no thought to what lies behind but push on to what is ahead. My entire attention is on the finish line as I run toward the prize to which God calls me- life on high with Jesus Christ. All of us who are spiritually mature must have this attitude."
>
> Philippians 3: 13-15

Let's remember that the great lessons we learned in our youth are just as important to apply in our daily lives today. When we come to the end of the line and have used up all of our allotted number of breaths, there will be no more chances for us. No more time for lamenting. No more, "If only I had done this or that, been kinder, helped others more, fought less, stopped lying, held my temper!" As we inch closer to our last step and ever nearer to our last breath in this life, we must be ready with our souls as pure as at the moment of Baptism and as innocent as when we took our first step in this world.

Consider these words from Sacred Scripture concerning the Final

Shut Up and Get in Line

Judgment:

"When the Son of Man comes as King and all the angels with Him, He will sit on his royal throne, and the people of all nations will be gathered before Him. Then He will divide them into two groups, just as a shepherd separates the sheep from the goats. He will put the righteous people at His right and the others at His left. Then the King will say to the people on His right, "Come, you that are blessed by My Father! Come and possess the kingdom which has been prepared for you ever since the creation of the world. I was hungry and you fed Me, thirsty and you gave Me a drink; I was a stranger and you received Me in your homes, naked and you clothed Me; I was sick and you took care of Me, in prison and you visited Me." The righteous will then answer Him, "When, Lord, did we ever see You hungry and feed You, or thirsty and give You a drink? When did we ever see You a stranger and welcome You in our homes, or naked and clothe You? When did we ever see You sick or in prison, and visit You?" The King will reply, "I tell you, whenever you did this for one of the least important of these brothers of Mine, you did it for Me!" Then He will say to those on His left, "Away from Me, you that are under God's curse! Away to the eternal fire which has been prepared for the Devil and his angels! I was hungry but you would not feed Me, thirsty but you would not give Me a drink; I was a stranger but you would not welcome Me in your homes, naked but you would not clothe Me; I was sick and in prison but you would not take care of Me." Then they will answer Him, "When, Lord, did we ever see You hungry or thirsty or a stranger or naked or sick or in prison, and would not help You?" The King will reply, "I tell you, whenever you refused to help one of these least important ones, you refused to help Me." These, then, will be sent off to eternal punishment, but the righteous will go to eternal life."

Matthew 25: 31-46

Whether you received your religious education from your parents, the priests, nuns and teachers, C.C.D., or some other source, continue learning our beautiful faith daily. There is so much to learn about our rich heritage. We can't neglect Prayer and the Sacraments. St. Thomas Aquinas instructs us- "Remember that the purpose of the sacraments is to help us on our way to our last end."[1] And St. Cyprian of Carthage warns us, "If He who was without sin prayed, how much more ought sinners to pray!"[2]

When the Final Judgment is complete and we have our assigned places for all eternity, I hope and pray that I see all of my relatives, the nuns and priests and teachers I knew, all my friends, John, Paul, Clair, Bob, Ralph, Babs, and classmates, all wearing the spotless raiment. And I really, really hope that they see me there too!

We don't want to go kicking and screaming into eternity. We need to tame our sharp tongues now. We really are brothers and sisters and in actuality are all connected. Not long ago, I could care less about anyone but myself. But now realizing that we are all related, I don't want any of us from Adam's Line to land in hell. I can picture our Lord saying to each one of us just as He said to Saint Gertrude, "Without you My Heaven would not be complete." Before we take that last step into our final destination, let's make sure our actions are in accord with the will

Shut Up and Get in Line

of our Creator by following His straight and narrow way and keeping His commandments now. Conformity to God's Holy will ensures the logical progression of our lives straight into the arms of our Heavenly Father.

If we have to bite our tongues to stop from offending Him, so be it. With all of our imperfections and scars, whether we have to limp or crawl in order to conform and get in line with His will, we must do whatever it takes. Every time we fall, we need to jump up and get right back in the race! And we mustn't forget to enlist the aid of our beautiful Mother. Saint Louis de Montfort reminds us—"Have you strayed from the path leading to heaven? Then call on Mary, for her name means 'Star of the Sea, the North Star which guides the ships of our souls during the voyage of this life,' and she will guide you to the harbor of eternal salvation."

When I was in high school I stood in a long line of girls against the wall in the hallway waiting to go to Confession. We stood in silence as Mother walked up and down the hallway. Mother was coming my way and getting very close to where I was standing, when a very surprising occurrence was going on at the other end of the line. As Mother was walking by me, I saw behind her that someone from way down the hall was flung out of line! She ran around in a circle after saving herself from hitting the opposite wall and tried desperately to find her spot again in line. She was scampering about fast and furious like a little mouse who was trying to find its way back to the hole in the wall. (I recognized the student as Regina, a fun-loving girl.) I could see the hysterics going on down the end of the corridor, but Mother had no idea. With Mother quickly approaching, I had to stifle my incurable laughter. Tears were rolling down my face and if poor Mother saw me crying, she probably thought I was contemplating my sins.

If we find ourselves out of line with God's perfect plan for our lives, we need to do as Regina did and find our way back at once! Not one second can be spared!

"Ultimately we all must learn the music of God- Silence- and we know its echo which is spiritual power that keeps us in tune and in perfect harmony with the Divine Musician."[3]

We must finish strong and be able to say what Saint Paul said, "I have fought the good fight, I have finished my course, I have kept the faith." Philippians 3:13-15.

Through the simple wisdom of the nuns, we learned deep theology by the mere act of patiently and silently standing in line.

Though vicious attacks from the evil one will continually assault you from all sides for the cherished prize of your God-given immortal soul, march on Heavenward in lockstep pace with Jesus, who escorts you, unflinching, supporting, defending, and loving you into His eternal Kingdom. He alone is "the narrow door," the One and Only Way through which we may enter. Don't wander off His straight and orderly path only to meet with disastrous consequences. Will we exclude ourselves because we are undisciplined and won't shut up? Will we continue to gossip, curse, lie or give into some other vile passion? When God's books are opened, every tongue will be silenced.

Silence comes with great rewards and brings us deeper into a loving relationship with the Lord. In Psalm 46:10, we learn the reason that silence is so critical. "Be still and know that I am God." "When our bodies become still and our minds become silent, God can achieve in us the greatest purification and transformation through the inflowing of divine love. In allowing ourselves just to (be) there for God- not doing anything, just being aware of His presence and allowing Him to heal and love us- receiving this love passively and surrounding our whole being to this powerful, silent, hidden, secret action of God, this type of prayer is of vital importance in our lives. St. John of the Cross verifies this when he says, "In contemplation the activity of the senses and of discursive reflection terminates and God alone is the agent Who then speaks secretly to the solitary and silent soul. Even though the soul is not doing anything, God is doing something in it."[4]

Remain sure-footed and take no chances since eternity is fast approaching, and indeed is in our midst. Remember the beauty and hidden value of silence. Stay in line and don't push anyone out! Rather, reach out and pull them in- as many as you can get, pull them all in! Use yourself as a living extension of Christ's life and love on earth as He gathers in His harvest. We need to offer prayers, encouragement and loving guidance to everyone.

As we stand at the crossroads between two worlds, the dividing line between time and eternity, we need to always keep our goal in mind and remember to thank God for those special warriors who have pointed us to the finish line. Our Lord's beloved servants, all His dedicated Priests, Nuns, Brothers, Deacons and everyone consecrated to divine service have given us immeasurable treasures in the lessons they taught us for this short life in preparation for the one that lasts forever. Praise God for preparing a place for your soul, and thank Him for those who helped prepare your soul for that place. Someday in the majestic beauty of Paradise, we may be able to thank all of them. But while we still walk this earth in anticipation of that glorious day when we are finally welcomed home by Our Lord and Savior, let's remember the passionate sense of urgency with which our great faith was passed on to us. It's not complicated. If we long to experience a wondrous eternity, we need only to put on our daily armor of Prayer, the Sacraments and Sacred Scripture and practice the beautiful character traits we learned in our youth.

Robert Cardinal Bellarmine tells us that "The school of Christ is the school of charity. On the last day, when the general examination takes place, there will be no question at all on the text of Aristotle, the aphorisms of Hippocrates, or the paragraphs of Justinian. Charity will be the whole syllabus."

We are all students in this worldwide school of love with our Divine Teacher inspiring His children to follow His irresistible light as He leads us onward and upward. Only through the power of Christ's love and mercy, and the generous outpouring of His graces, are hearts set on fire with holy zeal. A most mysterious and powerful change takes place in His children, strengthening them and emboldening them to get in line with His will. We need to cooperate with His graces and be self-disciplined.

Just as in the classrooms of our youth, some in our worldwide school will line up orderly and silently. Some will get in line slowly and begrudgingly. Then there are the rest of us, still loud, boisterous and out of control. Some of us need more assistance quieting ourselves. We're all in this together. Sometimes we need to help keep each other on track, and teach others through example the wonderful character traits we were taught. So, with steadfast Obedience, Self-Control, Perseverance, Cooperation, Courage and Orderliness, let us peacefully journey Heavenward together. Never forget the beautiful faith of our fathers that was passed down and entrusted to us. We must lovingly share it with others. Pray for those in religious life and always cherish the valuable, truthful and no-nonsense lessons we learned in school from the nuns and priests. We all have a vital role in the propagation of the faith. Many more workers are needed for the vineyard. We all must do our part in praying for vocations, so that all who hear "The Call" will faithfully answer.

While yearning to please our Heavenly Father, we may find ourselves resembling the same innocent little children that we were so many years ago.

> "Unless you become like little children, you will not enter the Kingdom of Heaven."
> Matthew 18:3-4

We have been taught our lessons well. So pay attention! Up straight! Move quickly and quietly, one behind the other! The storms and struggles of our daily lives will continue to assault us. We may lose our places; feel angry, lost, impatient, anxious or out of sync with God's perfect plan. Even so, we can always find our way back again if we just remember to shut up and get in line! We're going home!

NOTES

- Chapter 4- "Walking A Straight Line" – Conformity To God's Laws
  1. Saint Francis de Sales- The Dictionary of Quotes from the Saints, Paul Thigpen,(Ann Arbor, Michigan, Servant, 2001), 136
  2. Jeff Smith- Solid Food: Drawing Lines, www.watchmanmag. com/0610/061007.htm
  3. 3-Saint Alphonsus Liguori- Sermon on the Means Necessary for Salvation
  4. Jeff Smith- Solid Food: Drawing Lines, www.watchmanmag. com/0610/061007.htm
- Chapter 5- "God's Timeline" – Infinite Extension in Both Directions
  1. Catechism of the Catholic Church (Boston, MA., 1994),13
  2. Catechism of the Catholic Church (Boston, MA., 1994), 15
  3. Catechism of the Catholic Church (Boston, MA., 1994), 15
  4. Father John Laux, M.A.- Catholic Apologetics, Rockford, Illinois 1990,4-5
  5. Saint Alphonsus Liguori- Conformity to God's Will,1755- Translated by Thomas W.Tobin C.S.S.R.-1952
  6. Catechism of the Catholic Church (Boston, MA., 1994), 17
  7. Catechism of the Catholic Church (Boston, MA., 1994), 79
- Chapter 6- "Imaginary Lines" – Our Reader Friends
  1. Scott Foresman and Company's Publishing Timeline,

www.seriesbooks.com/dicktimeline
- Chapter 7- "Fall In Line" – "We're Headed Home"
  2. Jason Lisle, Ph.D.- God and Natural Law- Answers in Genesis, Aug. 28, 2006
  3. President Theodore Roosevelt- "A Textbook of Virtues"
  4. Father Stanley Jaki- The Biblical Basis of Western Science, Crisis 15, No. 9-1997,17-20-Father Jaki's lecture delivered in Philadelphia, Apr. 26, 1997
- Chapter 11- "Welcoming Line" – The Universal Church
  1. Jesus-Sacred Scripture, John 16:22
  2. Saint Theophane Venard- Thigpen,129
  3. Saint Francis of Assisi- Thigpen, 128
  4. Saint John Bosco- www.cfalive.org/St. JohnBosco
  5. Saint Theresa of Avila- Veritas Christi-The Truth of Christ, Perfecting the Four Temperaments, Part 2
  6. Saint Patrick- Saint Patrick's Breastplate-Catholic Prayers onlinewww.caholic.org/prayers
- Chapter 16- "God Writes Straight With Our Crooked Lines" – Some Family Nostalgia
  1. Patricia Kasten- The Compass, Official Newspaper of the Catholic Diocese of Green Bay- Foundations of Faith, Nov. 2, 2001 Issue.
  2. Kasten- Nov.2, 2001 Issue
  3. Kasten- Nov.2, 2001 Issue

- Chapter 17- "God's Plumb Line" – The Church
  1. Saint John of Damascus- Thigpen, 37
- Chapter 18- "Safety Line"- Family Loyalty

1. Louis Kaczmarek - "Hidden Treasure - The Riches of the Eucharist" - Trinity Communications, 1990- Manassas, VA, 55
2. Saint Thomas Aquinas- Thigpen, 39
- Chapter 19- "In the Line of Fire"- Hand Me Down Confirmation Name
  1. Saint Basil the Great- Thigpen, 117
- Chapter 22- "Line Of Demarcation" –Parent-Teacher Conference
  1. Saint Paul of the Cross- Thigpen, 52
- Chapter 23- "Smile Lines"- Ralph Cracks Up The Class
  1. Padre Pio- Thigpen, 132
- Chapter 24- "Every Cloud Has A Silver Lining" – May Procession
  1. Saint Gemma Galgani- Thigpen, 146
- Chapter 25- "Setting Boundary Lines" – Stay with The Program
  1. Saint Theresa of Lisieux- Thigpen, 221
- Chapter 26- "Top Of The Line Fashion For The In-Crowd"-Wearing White And Looking Good
  1. Saint John Vianney- Thigpen, 78
- Chapter 28- "On the Front Lines"- The Funniest Kid In The Class
  1. Father Benedict Groeschel, C.F.R.- The Cross at Ground Zero, Huntington, Indiana-2001, 74
  2. Father Groeschel, 72
  3. Father Groeschel, 58- 59
  4. Mother Theresa- www.largefamilylogistics.org, Life with Christ
- Chapter 31- "Our Lifeline" – The Holy Eucharist
  1. Saint Peter Julian Eynard- Champion of the Blessed Sacrament- Martin Dempsey, (Sentinel Press, 1964- New York) 286
  2. Saint Thomas Aquinas- Thigpen, 78

3. Saint Augustine- www.brainyquote.com/Augustine
4. Saint Thomas Aquinas- Catholic Encyclopedia- St. Thomas Aquinas
5. Louis Kaczmarek- "Hidden Treasure-The Riches of the Eucharist"- Trinity Communications, 1990-Manassas, VA,14,16
6. Louis Kaczmarek- Hidden Treasure-The Riches of the Eucharist"
7. Joan Carroll Cruz- "Eucharistic Miracles"- And Eucharist Phenomena in the Lives of the Saints"- Tan Books and Publishers, 1986-Rockford, Illinois, 205

- Chapter 33- "Lines Of Action"- A Few Catholics Who Shared Their Faith
    1. Cardinal Theodore McCarrick, Bob Hope- Catholic Standard- (Thinking of You, Aug. 7, 2003)
    2. Dion website-www.diondimucci.com
    3. Mel Gibson- Richard Salbato -www.unitypublishing.com/newletterGibsonLucia.htm
- Chapter 34- "What's My Line?"- Choose Your Service
    1. Saint Basil the Great- Thigpen, 16
    2. Saint Theresa of Avila- Thigpen, 31
- Chapter 37- "Are You Next In Line?" –Don't Get Ready, Be Ready!
    1. Saint Alphonsus Liguori- The Way of Salvation and of Perfection-(Brooklyn, 1926- Redemptorist Fathers), Meditation XXVI, 57 Matthew 25: 14-30
- Chapter 38- "Run Straight For The Goal Line" – Focus, Perseverance, Victory
    1. Saint Dominic- Thigpen, 158
    2. Saint Gregory of Nyssa- Thigpen, 158

3. Saint Alphonsus Liguori, Conformity to God's Will- www.stalphonsusbalt.org/conformity.htm, 4
4. Jesus, Sermon on the Mount
5. Saint Boniface- Thigpen, 37
6. Elizabeth Rundle Charles- The Best Loved Poems of the American People-Selected by Hazel Felleman, (Doubleday and Co., Garden City, N.Y.-1936) "The Child on the Judgment Seat"-331
7. Saint John of the Cross- Thigpen, 156
8. Saint Cyprian- Catholica.Pontifications.net

- Chapter 39- "Connecting Lines" – Jacob's Ladder
1. Saint Francis DeSales- Introduction to the Devout Life- Image Books, Doubleday-Dell, N.Y.,N.Y.,1972 The Nature and Excellence Of Devotion, Translated by John K. Ryan, Chapter 2.
2. Saint Augustine- The Columbia World of Quotations-196 #47914

- Chapter 42- "Crossing The Finish Line" – Out Of This World Family Reunion
1. Saint Cyprian-Catholica.Pontifications.net
2. St. Thomas Aquinas- Catholic Encyclopedia- St. Thomas Aquinas
3. "Reflections- The Nuns Today"- Talk given at the Monastery of St. Catherine of Siena- Dominican Family Day- June 30, 2007

www.ingramcontent.com/pod-product-compliance
Lightning Source LLC
LaVergne TN
LVHW011418080426
835512LV00005B/139